Traveling with the Coach

PEGGY ENGLISH

TRAVELING WITH THE COACH

To my five sons who traveled the road with us.

Contents

Wallace English Profile

S ummary of Experience

Over his career, Wallace coached four All-American quarterbacks: Dan Marino at University of Pittsburgh; Jim McMahon and Marc Wilson at Brigham Young University; and Don Strock at Virginia Tech. Overall, nine college quarterbacks that he personally coached were drafted into the National Football League. Four teams where he served as offensive coordinator led the NCAA Division I-A in passing.

Coaching profile

- University of Kentucky, Quarterback Coach
- University of Arkansas, Offensive Assistant and Offensive Line
- New Orleans Saints, Personnel Scout and Farm Club Coordinator, Richmond Roadrunners
- Virginia Technical University, Offensive Coordinator and Quarterback Coach
- University of Nebraska, Offensive Assistant and Quarterback Coach
- Detroit Lions, Running Backs Coach
- Brigham Young University, Offensive Coordinator and Quarterback Coach
- University of Pittsburgh, Offensive Coordinator and Quarterback Coach
- Miami Dolphins, Offensive Coordinator and Quarterback Coach
- Tulane University, Head Coach
- University of Hawaii, Offensive Coordinator
- Mt. Carmel High School, Houston, Texas, Head Coach
- Bishop Davis High School, Louisville, Kentucky, Head Coach
- Birmingham Bulls, European Professional League, Head Coach
- Palermo Cardinals, European Professional League, Head Coach
- Deggendorf Blackhawks, European Professional League, Head Coach
- Ohio Glory, World League of American Football, Offensive Coordinator
- World Football League, Eastern United States Personnel Coordinator

Playing experience

- · University of Louisville, Quarterback
- · Louisville United League, Quarterback
- · Fort Knox Post Team, All-Army League Quarterback

Forward

This book lets the readers travel with the English family through the twists and turns of what it was like "Traveling with the Coach." My dad passed away last summer (2024) at the age of 89. My mother is still working in the small consignment shop in Louisville, Kentucky.

My dad loved three things: his family, football, and all different kinds of foods. He was a tough father, only wanting for "his boys" to have a good home, a good school, good food and clothes, and to have some discipline in their lives: things he, himself, did not have growing up in the tough west end of Louisville. For him, sports were his way out and a way to better himself. He instilled that love of athletics in his sons. Even though we did not see much of him during the football season, my mother was always there to encourage and nurture all of us.

Even though "traveling with the coach" was at times hard on us kids—in the sense of leaving again after we had just made new friends and just learned about a new city—us "boys" had each other and could always count on Mom to hold it together while Dad was coaching. I'm sure moving around took a toll on us, but we all turned out okay. The Coach's boys are all successful in their own ways: one is a doctor, one is a lawyer, and three of us are in the construction industry. For the three in construction, we learned our trade from building our family homes with the Coach.

I'm sure our family's journey has been lived by many coaches' families. At times, I wouldn't wish it on anyone, but in a way, it was always exciting: lots of new and interesting people, lots of new and interesting places. Looking back, I wouldn't trade our family's travels with the coach for anything else.

For me and my brothers, there was always one truth—my dad loved his family—his heart was always in the right place. Much love to my mom and dad, for all they did for me and my brothers.

Jon English

Introduction

Who would have thought a little leather, elliptical ball would take me around the world? My husband was a football coach: nine colleges and three pro teams and seven European teams. His ability to teach young men how to throw and catch this pigskin took us to seventeen cities in the United States, including Hawaii, and moved us to seven different countries in Eastern and Western Europe.

We traveled to Japan to play in the Japan Bowl and played in a Super Bowl, Pro Bowl, Cotton Bowl, Fiesta Bowl, Gator Bowl, and Liberty Bowl, just to name a few.

All these stories that I have compiled and put in this book are true. They all occurred while traveling with the coach.

If I have counted correctly, we moved fifty-four times; I need to check the Guinness Book of Records. Each of the moves brought us laughs, trauma, excitement, and sometimes hysteria. We are like the mail: neither sleet, nor snow, nor rain or lost dog keeps us from moving, as you will learn in this book.

We have managed to have five sons along the way, raised them in many different cities and different schools. Each of the first four boys were left behind for their senior year of high school because they were valuable to their high school football team and did not want to move. All five received major college football scholarships, and three played pro football: one in the US and two in Europe.

One is a lawyer, one a doctor, and three are in the construction business. All this is from football. The funny thing is all five of them in the past have volunteered, in their spare time, to coach football. I suppose coaching gets into a family's blood.

As you can see, football has been good to us.

Wally started coaching in 1959, one week after we were married. Coaching then was not about money. Wally wanted to be a coach. My dad wanted him to go to law school, but he wanted to coach. Our first job paid $3,000.00 a year as an assistant. The next year, he got a head coach job in high school. It paid $3,300.00 a year for teaching and $400 for coaching. Three years later, he got another head coaching job in Texas. We made $7,000, We thought we had all the money in the world. When we went to Kentucky, we took a pay cut to get into college football. Wally never took a job for money; it was for a better position and a better team. The most we ever made was $70,000 as the head coach at Tulane. Wally had several assistant coaches—Bill Belichick, Joe Pendry, Bob Davie, and Mike Sherman, who all went on to be head coaches making a lot of money. He coached several quarterbacks that made it to the NFL. They all made good money.

Traveling with the coach helped me do several things: I wrote a book, *Real Women Know Football*. Because I would sit with the men after games and listen to the conversation, a lady said to me, "I want to learn about football, so I can talk about it also." So I started teaching women about football; thus, it turned into a book. I was able to go on *The View*, *Good Morning America*, many radio shows in many cities doing their morning shows, and a lot of book signings. I had my own TV show, *Real Women Know Football*. I started a football jewelry company and did National Champion pins for LSU, Ohio State, and Alabama.

While living in Hawaii, I started a TV Series, *Romance in Football*, having famous sports couples tell their own stories.

I started the first espresso coffee shop in Louisville, Kentucky, because after coaching in Italy, when we came home, there was not a good coffee shop. It was about a year before Starbucks, and I saw a need for a good coffee shop like the ones we got to experience overseas, especially in Italy.

All this because of traveling with the coach.

We have lived in fifty different houses. We seemed to move as each of our boys reached their senior year in high school. Jon stayed behind at Brother Rice High School in Detroit; Steve had to move to Pittsburgh from BYU in Utah. Dan stayed behind in Miami at St. Thomas Aquinas High School, and Tom stayed behind in New Orleans at Jesuit High School. They were all starting quarterbacks for their schools. Our youngest son, Andrew, was in three different high schools, and he was always the starting quarterback. All five of our sons received major college quarterback scholarships.

Early Years

We were married on July 25, 1959. When we got married, our honeymoon was just like our life. We just started out driving with a few places in mind: Chicago; the Green Bay Packers training camp; Traverse City, Michigan; and back to Louisville, Kentucky. We continued this pattern for all of married life: a few places in mind, many stops along the way. To be married to a football coach was adventuresome. Well, I would say much more to me than him.

Wally only wanted boys. It's a good thing that is what we were blessed with. Our first son was born in 1960. It was the day of my husband's first game as head coach against St. Joseph Prep in Bardstown, Kentucky; he came to the hospital on the team bus and came up to check on me. Of course, the bus was full of players, and they kept shouting, "Hurry up, Coach!"

Our second son was born while Wally was playing in a game as quarterback in the Continental League. When he got home and found the babysitter there, he was furious, thinking that I was out playing bridge. The sitter said, "No, she is at the hospital having a baby."

I was induced with our third son because Wally had taken a job in Houston. As soon as our son was born, Wally then left for Texas.

Our fourth son was born during a big weekend of recruiting. I had lots of labor pains during Mass, then I went home to find recruits at our house. I decided to wait until they were gone before leaving for the hospital. Once I got to the hospital, the baby was born in about an hour. To play a joke on Wally, the nurses wrapped our new baby boy in a pink blanket, trying to fool Wally into thinking it was a girl!

Our fifth and final son's birthday was picked by Don Shula. Wally had taken a job with the Miami Dolphins. Coach Shula said he could come home for one day, March 26, so Andrew was born on that day. I know today that is hard to believe, but that was the way it was when Wally was coaching. Football dictated even when your children were born.

Mount Carmel

Wally left as soon as Danny was born to take a high school job in Houston, Texas. This job paid $7,000. I could not believe it. That was all the money in the world. Jon (four), Steve (three), Danny (one month), and I left on the boys' first airplane ride. I had Jon hold onto one side of my skirt and Steve hold onto the other side; I carried Dan in a basket.

Wally had not found a house yet. The one he liked had a six-foot fence around the backyard. The boys would not get out. Mount Carmel paid for an apartment for us to rent until we found a house. It was on the second floor with a very small rail around it and walk-up stairs to the apartment. I could not let the boys out because below was a large swimming pool. I found a house very quickly. The house needed work, so before we moved, Wally got the football team to come over to paint the inside and fix the yard. It was great!

The boys and I shopped a lot. Houston was such a big city compared to Louisville, Kentucky, but I could take the boys downtown, and we could wander through all the stores. I would hear over the loudspeaker, "Mrs. English, you are lost, and your son is looking for you." I once took them into a very exclusive store—what did I know? After a few minutes, a lady asked me if I wanted to come back when I did not have my children. Lesson learned.

It was exciting living in Houston, especially at Christmas. The decorations were over the top: one house had a very large Christmas tree, twenty feet tall, decorated to the nines. Underneath was a new Thunderbird wrapped with a ribbon. I decided to go to Niemen Marcus to buy Wally a gift, just to say it came from Niemen's, as the natives called it. I bought him a gold wristwatch. The lady said they would deliver it after they engraved Wally's initials on the back.

A black limo pulled up to the house, just as Wally was coming home from practice. The chauffeur handed the wrapped gift to Wally. He opened it and was very pleased. He asked me how much.

"$45," which at that time, was a lot of money.

"$45," he said, "but there is no guarantee with it."

The next day, I called the store clerk who sold me the watch. I explained the situation. In icicle tones, she said, "My dear, does it have Niemen Marcus's name on it?"

I said yes.

She said, "That is all the guarantee you need," and hung up.

We still have the watch.

Miscellaneous Anecdotes

You have a ready-made family when you move from one football team to another, ready-made friends. All the coaches' wives accept you and try to help you. I always stress this in my speeches: moving is easy because of this. Because my sons were all good athletes, they also had ready-made families in their schools, and of course because their father was a coach, everyone wanted to know them.

So many funny things I remember, especially about my children.

Tom was three; he fell and cut himself. It was at night, so I grabbed an old coat and scarf and took him to the emergency room. I knew it didn't look very good; I heard them ask Tommy if I had hit him or knocked him down.

When our son, Andrew, was born fourteen years after Tommy, Wally had already gone to Miami. Andrew was sent home in Pampers. Well, after so many years, I did not know that pampers were a new thing. I ordered cloth diapers and threw away the Pampers. After about a week, I noticed Andrew had red spots on his stomach, so off we went to the doctor. The doctor took a look and said to me, "Do you smoke?"

"No." I replied, and he then asked, "Then you did not burn him with a cigarette?"

I was horrified. The doctor said he had to ask. He decided the red spots were from the diapers! No more diaper service: back to the Pampers.

I believe I spent more time in doctors' offices with those five boys. Of course, Wally was rarely there. That's the way it was when traveling with the coach.

Part 1: Colleges & Pro Teams

University of Kentucky: 1965-68

T he University of Kentucky was one of the most interesting places where Wally coached. From Mo Moorman running down University Drive screaming "I'm not going to take that!" to Charlie Bradshaw having a fence built around the practice field with curtains to keep photographers from taking pictures of the players (or pictures of the coaches punching the players), there were certainly a lot of things happening in those days in Lexington. Bill Conde was an interesting character; so were a lot of young men associated with the program. Charlie Bradshaw, the head coach, was the most interesting of all the coaches. The defense coaching staff included Bill "Moon" Conde, defensive coordinator; Charlie Pell, defensive line coach; Leon Fuller, defensive backfield coach; and Doug Shively, defensive end coach. On the offensive side, Wally English was the quarterback coach; Jimmy Poynter coached the running backs; and George Sengel was the offensive line and receivers' coach. Coach Bradshaw had a concrete stage where he lectured and conducted business every practice. The staff reported to work every day at 7:30 a.m. Coach Bradshaw would talk about what the day's practice was going to be about. He would read the categories—they were usually the same every day, about two hours of fun from the time it started until the time it ended.

Coach Paul "Bear" Bryant had been the coach at Kentucky and successful in the 1940s and early 1950s. Those were good times for Kentucky Wildcats football. Coach Bryant left U of K to coach at Texas A&M when the boosters gave Adolph Rupp a new Cadillac car and gave Coach Bryant a cigarette lighter for their Christmas bonuses. Coach Charlie Bradshaw accepted the head coaching job in 1962 from Athletic Director Bernie Shively after Shively fired Blanton Collier, who went on to coach the Cleveland Browns in the NFL. You may recall, if you followed football in those days, that this was the year of the "Thin Thirty" in Kentucky football, when Bradshaw thinned the team from 88 to 30 players. Even though those were not our happiest days, Wally was glad to be there and learned a lot of football.

We had just moved to Kentucky, had not gotten paid yet, and did not have much money when the coaches' wives got together. Each brought a dish. I was asked to bring potato chips, 59¢. I had to go through pockets and piggy banks to come up with 59¢.

We built our first house in Lexington. It was a 3,600-square-foot Georgia Colonial, and it backed up to a park. We were directly across the street from the head of the Department of Dentistry. Wally was making the "big bucks." After he was promoted to the full-time position of quarterback coach, we were making, as I recall, $7,500 a year. In fact, I went with Wally when we were attempting to buy the building lot from a man, a land developer, who luckily happened to be a big Kentucky football booster. His name was Mr. Martin. Wally introduced himself as the new quarterback coach on Charlie Bradshaw's staff and said we really liked the area and this particular lot of land. Wally proceeded to ask him how much the lot was. Mr. Martin said that the lot cost $35,000. Wally said that was very reasonable and that we wanted to purchase it.

Then Mr. Martin said that because Wally was a U of K coach, he would actually sell it to us for $25,000. This was even better. Then came the problem: Mr. Martin wanted to know how much we could put down. He asked $1,000, to which we replied we could not; then he asked about $500 down, and again we had to say we couldn't afford that either. Wally finally asked Mr. Martin if he would accept $100 down on the lot. Mr. Martin accepted with one condition: he said that we had to build a really nice house here, which we both promised.

The next day, armed with five or six pencils and some string, we went and laid out the area where we intended to build the house. We went to a student in the architectural studies department and had him draw up the plans for our new house. This was after spring practice, so we had the entire summer to construct our dream home.

Let me tell you about some of the trips that I was allowed to take with him when he was either recruiting or scouting. I remember going with Wally to New Orleans when he was scouting LSU vs. Tulane. We arrived in New Orleans on Friday, and the game was not to be played until Saturday night in the old Tulane Stadium. That gave us some time on Saturday to look around New Orleans because neither of us had been there before. There was a great restaurant in the French Quarter called Brennan's. We found the place in an old pink building. We were greeted at the door by the maître d', who was dressed in a tux. In fact, all the waiters had on tuxes. We were shown to a table in a lovely garden. The waiter brought the menu, and it was written mostly in French. We did, with some help, find flamed grapefruit, eggs Benedict, sautéed chicken breast, French bread, and some sort of drink with a little paper parasol in it. Then for dessert, we had bananas foster. It was delicious, a wonderful breakfast. When the bill came, it was $18.00; with tip, it was over $20.00, and after parking, breakfast cost over $25.00, which back in those days was big bucks. When we got back to Lexington and Wally turned his expense report, Coach Bradshaw called him into his office and said, "Coach, I understand; I've been to Brennan's before. Please change this $25.00 for your breakfast to your cost for dinner that day." That was our first trip to New Orleans, our first time at Brennan's, and Wally's first time to be called into Charlie Bradshaw's office for overspending.

Back in those days, the NCAA was not as strict on spending. There were not as many rules. Coaches, when they were on the road, could pretty much eat any place they chose as long as they could bring back a receipt from that restaurant. Wally, for his dinner meals when he was on the road, ate in some lovely and expensive restaurants. He would always ask for a menu, so he could bring it home to me, and I could see where he had eaten. Pretty soon, I had a large stack of menus from all over the country. The next house we built, I simply wallpapered our entry hall bathroom with the menus. That brought lots of comments from our house guests.

I am not certain that I should include these stories in the book, but what the heck. It's been over fifty years, so here it goes. I am not always certain of the years; I only have some notes which I kept when Wally would call me from the road. I do remember that Kentucky was about to play the University of Missouri [MU] on the road to open the 1965 season. Wally was sent to MU by Charlie Bradshaw about three weeks before the game to get a little information on the Tigers' offense and defense. Wally would call me at night and tell me about his day. Once he arrived in Columbia, Missouri (which is halfway between St. Louis and Kansas City), Wally found that the stadium was under renovation. The University of Missouri football practice field was immediately adjacent to the stadium. As Wally drove past the practice field, many students and football student managers saw him and yelled "Spy! Spy! Spy!" Wally knew he had to find someplace where he could see Missouri practice.

He looked around the big campus and spotted a tall building, which he approached, and found it to be the girls' dormitory. Even though the football team was practicing, the campus was still empty. School wasn't in session for another three weeks. Wally parked his car about two blocks away from the dormitory and walked over to the building. He got on the elevator and went to the top floor. He was able to see the Tigers practice from about two blocks away until again he saw some students pointing toward him and starting to run toward the girls' dormitory. Wally was able to make a hasty retreat and get out of the dormitory without being captured. The next day, Wally drove his car into Columbia. He found a resale shop where he bought some old work boots and a hard hat, a tape measure, and a tool belt. He was now prepared to enter the stadium as a worker.

Even though there was a guard checking people coming and going into the stadium, Wally was able to get past him. Upon entering the stadium, Wally found a place to watch from high above the practice field. It was on a stairway with an opening in the wall. He stood there with his tape measure in hand just in case someone came up the steps. He was able to make mental notes about Missouri's offense and defense. This was during two-a-day practices. As Missouri finished the morning practice, Wally was now confronted with the problem of getting out of the stadium. Luckily, some of the workers were leaving for lunch, so Wally just joined in with them, and he went back to his motel and put the mental notes onto paper. Wally got some lunch, went back to the stadium, watched the afternoon practice, and then went back and checked out of the motel. Upon leaving, the lady at the desk said, "I see that you're from Lexington, Kentucky. What are you doing out here?"

Wally replied, "Oh, we build silos. We are getting ready to build some big silos just down the road here."

"That's good. I thought you might be one of those Kentucky Wildcats," the lady said.

"I wish I was, but I'm just an old silo builder. Thanks, ma'am. I sure enjoyed your motel," Wally replied.

If you look back at the records from the 1965 UK versus MU game, Kentucky beat Missouri in that season opener. Missouri did not lose many more games that year. Wally drove back to Kentucky and resumed his coaching duties. This is probably the first and only time this has ever been revealed.

I hope that my good friend, Barbara Dooley, will forgive me when I tell this story about our husbands. In 1965, Kentucky beat Georgia in Lexington and scored twenty-eight points in the second quarter. Wally was sent to scout Michigan versus Georgia in Ann Arbor, Michigan. It turns out that Wally was staying in the same Holiday Inn that the University of Georgia was staying in, too. It was a daytime game. Wally was just going down for breakfast when he saw the team preparing to leave after their pregame meal. He saw Coach Vince Dooley toss his room key onto the table where he had just eaten his meal. After Georgia left the hotel on buses for the stadium, Wally walked over to Coach Dooley's table and picked up the room key that Vince had left. After the Georgia team was safely out of sight, Wally went back to Vince's room and found a torn-up game plan and taped the three-page game plan together.

In those days, at Kentucky, each of the ten assistant coaches was assigned an opponent to scout. George "Chink" Sengel was assigned to scout Georgia. If the Kentucky Wildcats won the game you were assigned to scout, you received a $100 gift card to Dawahares men's store in Lexington. Kentucky beat Georgia. Chink got a new suit. I'm not certain anyone ever knew Wally had gotten Vince's game plan. Espionage.

Indiana University had a really good year when John Pont was the coach. It was 1967, and Kentucky was to open with this tough opponent. Someone sent Wally on a covert mission; I think it was probably Charlie Bradshaw. Again, it was two or three weeks before the opening game. Wally arrived in Bloomington, Indiana. He rode around the practice field. There was a building under construction immediately across the street from the practice facility. It must've been a Saturday or something because Wally told me no one was in the new building. He parked the car three blocks away, walked back, and got on the second floor of the building. He could not see. He then walked to a wooded area behind the practice field. The Hoosiers were scrimmaging. The chain-link fence had plastic strips. Again, Wally could not see from ground level in the woods. He climbed a tree. He had on his good dress clothes and a brand-new pair of shoes. This was a big sacrifice for the good of the team. Wally was in the tree making mental notes when the branch he was standing on broke. Wally fell onto Indiana's practice field. He said, "To hell with the new shoes; to hell with the dress clothes; I'm getting the hell out of here!" He climbed to the top of the fence, tore his pants, scuffed his shoes, ran through the woods, and luckily got away. Wally probably did not have enough time to get enough information because, as I recall, Indiana won the opener against Kentucky, 12–10.

Another time, Wally was gone recruiting, and I became ill with the flu. I had a baby to take care of. I made a pallet on the floor and put the baby in a playpen. I got so weak I could not fix any food. I called a neighbor whom I did not know very well to see if she would come help me; the kids and I were on the floor with empty cans of soup. The place was a mess. The neighbor came and cleaned up and washed the baby; she told the rest of the neighborhood women that I was a drunk. Finally, one of the other coach's wives came over and took me to the hospital.

We always had a lot of kids at the house. One morning, Wally was home, and we had a few extra kids for breakfast. The boys introduced their friends. That night for dinner, Wally was home early; he asked, "Who are these new boys?" Jon said, "Don't you remember? They were here for breakfast." The life of a coach during the season: always distracted. Their minds are always on football.

Another time Wally was recruiting, he was to be gone two weeks. It snowed in Lexington, so all the neighbors got together, and we had a bonfire while the kids sleighed. Someone threw a paint can in the fire, and it exploded. Jon was right by it, and it burned the first layer of skin. Luckily, a doctor lived next door. He put ointment on Jon's face. We did not tell Wally because he could not come home, and he could not do anything, so two weeks went by, and Wally came home. Jon's face was red, but that was about all.

I rarely told Wally when the boys got hurt because he would get so upset. I learned that very early. When Jon was about three, he swallowed some lighter fluid. I rushed him to the doctor, and they pumped his stomach. I thought they were very rough on Jon. I made the mistake of calling the football office and telling Wally I was upset with the doctor. The other coach said Wally got up, threw his keys across the room, let out a few profanities, went to the doctor's office, and cussed him out.

Another time, our son, Dan, fell and cut his arm quite badly. Wally was across the street; I called him to come over. He put a tourniquet on the wound. I called EMS. They were very slow in responding. Wally called and cussed them out; he then took Dan to the emergency room.

A couple more stories before we leave Kentucky...

I was in the grandstands to see this personally: it happened in the old Stoll Field in Lexington. The University of Kentucky was playing the University of Mississippi. John Vaught was the coach at Ole Miss. They were a good team. As I recall, Mississippi had a really good defense. They kept tackling Dicky Lyons in the backfield. For a long time, Dicky Lyons led the nation in kickoff and punt returns. He had those records for years. Anyhow, the situation arose: Ole Miss was on defense. They had Kentucky backed up. It was fourth down and 43 yards to go for a first down. It was late in the third quarter, and the game was on the line. Wally was the kicking coach; Larry Seiple was the punter. The ball was snapped. Seiple held the ball; he did not punt. He started to run. You must understand this: Charlie Bradshaw was not a nice man when we lost. From where I sat in the stands, I could see Wally in the press box. He was usually seated, but when Seiple started to run, Wally stood up and took off his headset. I presumed he did not want anyone to hear what he was saying.

Ole Miss was executing a punt return. They had started setting up a wall. It was amazing to watch. The wall of blockers was approximately on the hash mark, where they were planning for their punt return man to catch the ball and run between the wall of blockers and the sideline for a lot of yardage or even a touchdown. But that was not what I was seeing. Seiple was running behind the Ole Miss wall. No one could be that stupid to attempt to make a first down when the downwind distance was fourth and 43. I was looking at the field, then I was looking at Wally in the press box. At first, it appeared Wally was saying "No, Larry, no, Larry." Now, he appeared to be saying "Go, Larry, go, Larry. That a boy, Larry!"

The original line of scrimmage on fourth down was probably about the Kentucky 25-yard line. Now Seiple had traveled to approximately midfield and was crossing into Ole Miss territory. Just as Seiple started to get close to the first down marker, an Ole Miss tackler grabbed him, but Larry wiggled across the line for a first down. That play was the turning point in the game.

Kentucky beat a heavily favored Ole Miss team 16 to 7. Wally told me when they got to the dressing room, Coach Bradshaw called him and Larry Seiple to speak with him. Charlie said, "Great job, Larry and Wally. But Wally, it's a damn good thing that it worked."

Wally had two good recruiting areas: he recruited Louisville and Cincinnati for Kentucky. If Kentucky was playing at home, Wally would usually drive to Louisville to watch some Friday night football games. Usually the game would be over about ten o'clock. Wally would go to Hasenour's restaurant; that was where most of the high school coaches would go after the games. It gave Wally a little insight into what had happened in the other high school games which he had not seen. He would then drive back to Lexington and usually get home about one or two o'clock in the morning.

You may have heard about Kentucky revenue officers chasing moonshine distillers. Wally said he would drive from Louisville to Lexington on Interstate 64 East when he came to Frankfurt and crossed over the Kentucky River. He could smell the moonshiners' stills cranking out that white lightning. Back in those days, a lot of automobiles did not have air conditioning, so you rode along with your windows down. He said for about ten miles, there in those hills around Frankfurt, you could smell the stills producing mountain whiskey.

Wally, because of his Friday night drives from Lexington to Louisville back to Lexington, was able to sign some pretty good high school football players to become Kentucky Wildcats. Wally signed Nate Northington, a running back from Thomas Jefferson High School in Louisville, and the first African American to play college football in the Southeastern Conference. Wally also signed Greg Page; they were the first two African American players to attend the University of Kentucky. Unfortunately, Greg passed away after being paralyzed from a neck injury during a UK practice in 1967. It was ironic that he passed away the day before Nate integrated the SEC. It was so sad.

In October or November, just after we had moved into the newly built house and were becoming comfortable, Wally came home and handed me a note. He said that we needed to start packing again. Coach Bradshaw had just resigned, and Wally was fired! That'll take the wind out of your sails.

Luckily, a friend of ours from Houston, a coach by the name of J.D. Roberts, had just come through Lexington scouting the Wildcats team for NFL prospects for the New Orleans Saints. We had not been fired for a week when J.D. Roberts called and said that he was going to coach the Richmond Roadrunners, a farm club team for the New Orleans Saints and the Los Angeles Rams. We put our beautiful brand-new dream home on the market. In total, after completion, we had $36,000 invested in the house. It was truly beautiful. Within a month, we were preparing to move to Richmond, Virginia. We received an offer of $48,000 for our dream house, so we were fortunate with both the house and the new job.

New Orleans Saints & Richmond Roadrunners: 1969

We loved Richmond. The only bad part about the job: Wally had to be a personnel scout for the Saints in the spring and the offensive coordinator for the Richmond Roadrunners in the fall.

It did not take us long to find a nice new house on a lake just outside of Richmond, across the river in beautiful Henrico County, Virginia. It was a great neighborhood. I had lots of lady friends who kept me company while Wally was on the road scouting for players for the Saints.

I can still remember one strange early incident: because we had not sold our house in Lexington yet, and because Wally was only in Richmond during the season, he stayed in the stadium. We had a car in Lexington which we wanted to take to Richmond, so one weekend, I left Lexington and headed for Richmond on a Friday. Wally had a Saints company car, but we wanted to get this Buick to Richmond. It was about a ten-hour drive in those days; I-64 had not been totally completed.

I had my hair fixed. I had a pretty new dress. I was going to see my honey for the weekend. When I arrived in Richmond, the electricity in Wally's space was off. The only electricity in the stadium was in the dressing room. This was in the off-season, so the dressing room was not in use. The only bed which we could find were the tables in the training room. The lights, which we could not turn off, were the lights from the Coke machine. I could still remember sitting on the training table with a sheet pulled around me, watching the roaches crawl on the training room floor. We could've stayed in a Holiday Inn, but Wally being the good guy that he is said, "Oh, no. Again, I can stay in the stadium." Never again, never again.

Wally told me a story about J.D. Roberts. J.D. was a tough dude. He had been an offensive lineman for the University of Oklahoma when Bud Wilkinson had been the head coach there and had won fifty games in a row. The Richmond Roadrunners played in City Stadium in Richmond. J.D. was a stickler for field maintenance. Other events were scheduled in the stadium from time to time. Once, the city of Richmond scheduled some sort of a circus on the game field. J.D. was beside himself; he was angry. Wally and J.D. called the stadium manager to come to the field. The manager showed up with his enormous German Shepherd dog. The dog was obviously the stadium manager's protector. The manager knew Coach Roberts did not agree with a circus tearing up the football field. The manager surely had been confronted by others in the past. There was a little area where he could pull up against the fence, and the only way you could speak to him was through the dog. That didn't bother J.D. at all. J.D. went right up to the pickup truck's window with the dog growling and started speaking harshly to the stadium manager. The big dog bit J.D. right on his left forearm. Wally said J.D. did not even wince or break the continuity of his sentence. He just kept right on speaking.

Obviously, the dog had never seen anything like that before. The dog crawled backwards inside the truck, the manager fixed the field, and everything was okay. However, what Wally had just seen with J.D. and the dog made Wally think J.D. was the toughest man he had ever seen.

By this time, our family was growing. We now had Jon, who was in the fourth grade, Steve, who was in the second grade, and Danny was a baby. Wally being gone all the time got old to me and the coach, so when Wally was offered the position of assistant offensive line coach at Arkansas, we accepted immediately.

The University of Arkansas: 1969-70

Wally was getting established and recognized as a good of-
fensive-minded coach, but a coaching career can be a difficult and fickle one. We had just finished the season with the
Richmond Roadrunners, and even though we loved Richmond,
the NFL's associations with farm clubs were coming to an end.
We were, once again, looking for the next stop on our coaching
trek. Wally had been offered a management job by Max Pierson,
the owner of Richmond Chrysler/Plymouth and owner of the
Richmond Roadrunners. Max and his wife Billie had become
friends of Wally and me. However, Wally wanted to stay in
coaching, so we decided to ask Frank Broyles if we could join his
staff at the University of Arkansas as a Graduate Assistant [GA].

Wally borrowed a Richmond Chrysler/Plymouth company
car from Max and drove from Richmond, Virginia, to Fayetteville, Arkansas, to talk to Frank Broyles. When Wally arrived
in Fayetteville, he found that Coach Broyles was at a Southwest
Conference meeting at Texas Tech in Lubbock. So off again
to Texas Tech. The meeting was being held in the downtown
Holiday Inn. Wally went to the Holiday Inn and found Coach
Broyles. Coach Broyles was impressed that Wally would take a
chance to drive halfway across the country in hopes of getting

to meet with him. After a brief visit, Broyles invited Wally to join the staff as a GA. He told Wally to go back to the University and find Coach Merv Johnson.

Once back in Fayetteville, Wally found Merv, who made arrangements for Wally and me to rent a university-owned apartment. Wally was to make $118 a month as a GA. Once back in Richmond, we closed up our house and stored our furniture in a neighbor's basement. We had to rent a trailer, clean out the house, and start back to Fayetteville. It was so close to school starting, there wasn't anywhere to live. Our only option was to move into the apartments for married students. We left a 2,800 square-foot home for a 300 square-foot apartment.

Even though the apartment was not very big, we made the best of it and had fun. The apartment complex was like the United Nations, in the sense that we had Chinese, Japanese, American Indian, African, and more all in the complex. I always thought it was a good experience for my sons to be exposed to and interact with so many different cultures. The apartment was not very big, but Wally, the boys, and I made the best of it. The boys, Jon and Steve, became regular visitors to the recreation center in the neighborhood.

There was still some time before practice and the season started, so Coach Broyles assigned each coach an area to recruit. Wally got Houston. We had a car that my father, J.P. Karem, had given us. It was an Oldsmobile and a good driving car on the road. It was about 500 miles from Fayetteville to Houston. The athletic association paid Wally $0.15 a mile to drive his own car on the road in recruiting. The extra money came in very helpful with our expenses. Wally made three or four recruiting trips to Houston and brought some really good prospects to Arkansas, including an all-NFL prospect who got away and went to SMU. The trips to Houston generated about $500.00 profit for food and other expenses. Coach Broyles liked the prospects Wally brought to Arkansas.

For a young coach, college football season goes year-round. If you are not coaching, you are recruiting. You are reviewing films of players, working on playbooks, or going to coaching clinics. For Wally, it was a whirlwind of experience. For me and the boys, it was trying to develop a routine, kind of like Maria in *The Sound of Music*. We had fun finding new adventures in all the various towns along the way. Wally was big on education, so we were always trying to locate the family close to the best schools and neighborhoods we could find. Looking back, Arkansas was a good experience for our family. Wally was busy, and the boys and I had a good support system from the other coaches' wives and their children. That was the good thing about coaching: most of the time we had a built-in support system from the other wives who were in the same boat.

As time grew near for fall practice to begin, Wally was assigned to help Merv Johnson with the offensive line. Wally felt this was a really good thing because he had not had much experience with linemen. Since line pass protection was so important, Wally learned a lot about protecting the quarterback on pass plays. Because of this, Coach Broyles wanted Wally to coach Joe Ferguson, the Razorback backup quarterback, some and add his expertise to help fellow coach, Don Breaux, with his techniques. Wally did that in addition to his offensive line coaching duties. Coach Broyles felt Wally did a good job in both areas he was assigned. Due to his experience with signals and signaling plays from the sideline to the quarterback on the field, Coach Broyles asked Wally to be a signaler on the sideline for the Razorbacks. Coach Breaux was in the press box calling the plays, and Merv Johnson and Wally were on the sidelines signaling to the quarterback what Breaux had called from the press box. This was a big responsibility.

Now that he was a signaler, Wally got to travel with the team to every game. Being part of a Division 1 major college team, many things are learned: bed checks, eating protocols, bus-riding organization, etc. Wally was appreciative to Coach Broyles and gave his complete loyalty to the coach and the program.

As I look back, the thing I remember about the first Arkansas football game is thinking I should go to the store so that we would have food for after the game. I went downtown to shop, and every single grocery, bank, and shop were closed. I did not realize how important game day was in Fayetteville.

The Razorbacks won nine games that year and finished 7th in the AP Top 25 poll. The team was selected to go to the Sugar Bowl to play a very good Ole Miss team with a QB named Archie Manning. It was our family's first bowl experience of many to come. I remember Wally was given a Rolex watch as part of the bowl gift package.

He still wears it to this day.

After the season was over, coaches were given a week or so off to relax at home with their families. Once again, Coach Broyles assigned Wally to scout the Houston area. Wally was glad, as he was familiar with the area. There were lots of good players in Texas that year, especially in the Houston area. Every weekend, Arkansas would have recruits visit the campus to watch the basketball games and allow the coaches to see the prospects personally. Wally had a lot of good prospects come from Houston to visit the Arkansas campus. Coach Broyles was pleased with his recruiting efforts.

Since Arkansas had been successful that year, several Arkansas assistants were offered head-coaching positions at various universities. Coach Broyles was always very positive about his assistant coaches, and many of his assistant coaches from Arkansas became head coaches at good universities. While there, I had a chance to meet one of my best friends, Sally Berry, the wife of UA wide receivers coach Raymond Berry, who had been the outstanding Hall of Fame NFL receiver with the Baltimore Colts. Wally knew Johnny Unitas, the Colts' quarterback, very well, so it was easy for us to get to know Sally and Raymond. Raymond left UA to coach with the Detroit Lions.

During the offseason, as recruiting was progressing, there was a lull in all the offseason activity. Coach Broyles called Wally into his office and gave him some fatherly advice. He said, "You should do this, you should not do this. Someday you will be a head coach, and you will want to look for these traits in your own assistant coaches." Wally thanked Coach Broyles and did a graceful exit from the office. It was not until later that Wally found out that Coach Broyles had recommended him to Charlie Coffey, the UA defensive coordinator.

Wally was recruiting in Texas and made his daily call into the office. The secretary asked Wally to call Charlie Coffey. Wally called Charlie, who in short order asked Wally if he'd like to go to Virginia Tech with him and coach the running backs. Charlie told Wally he'd pay him as much as he could, probably around $25,000. Wally said, "Yes coach, thank you." Charlie told Wally to come home from Texas, and Coach Broyles was on board with it all. So we got the VT job over the phone somewhere outside Houston, Texas.

That day, Wally called me from a pay phone in Texas. You must remember: in those days, people did not have cell phones. He asked me, "How would you feel about going back to Virginia?"

"Oh, no! We've been there and done that," I said. "What's the matter, did you get fired?" I asked.

"No," he said, "our defensive coordinator, Charlie Coffey, just accepted the Virginia Tech coaching job, and he wants me to go with him and coach the running backs. He even told me to call Coach Broyles to ask his opinion before I gave him an answer.

When I called Broyles, he said to do it! So," he said to me, "if you want to go back, start packing."

"Hey!" I said. "Wait a minute, if you are going to be the back-field coach, they should move us!"

"Oh, yeah," he said. "I forgot to tell you: Charlie said that Virginia Tech would take care of all the moving. Charlie is in Blacksburg right now recruiting, and he wants me to drive his pickup from Fayetteville to meet him. Virginia Tech will fly you and the kids there as soon as I find us a place to live."

"Will they move our furniture from Richmond to Blacksburg?" I asked, hopeful.

Wally assured me that it would not be a problem, so I started tying up loose ends once again, and off we went to Blacksburg and Virginia Tech.

Virginia Tech: 1971-72

When we were coaching at University of Kentucky, I remember one of the wives talking about how Blacksburg,
Virginia, was the most backwoods place they had ever coached,
but Blacksburg is a beautiful little town. Back in those days, it
had a population of only thirteen thousand people, not count-
ing the students. If you're familiar with that part of Virginia, it's
close to Roanoke. You may remember that the old VPI, Virginia
Polytechnic Institute, has a long and storied history dating from
Civil War times as a military school. It is very picturesque; it has
old colonial-looking stone buildings. It is set in the rolling hills
southwest of Roanoke and directly west of Christiansburg, Virginia. It is not far north of the North Carolina state line. We decided since we still owned the house in Richmond, and since all
our furniture was there, it would be a good idea for the children
and I to return there so that they could finish the school year
with their old classmates. We felt it would be difficult for them
to start in the middle of a school year with new teachers and
new classmates. Wally explained this to Charlie, and he agreed.

Charlie had two cars and a truck. Wally drove Charlie's truck
to Blacksburg. When he got to Blacksburg, he bumped into an
old U of K player named Luke Lynch. Luke had an empty barn

and said that we could put our furniture in it until we had a house.

Wally would go through spring practice, try to find a house or lot, and make the necessary preparations for us to move from Richmond to Blacksburg. He was allowed to come back to Richmond to help us get the furniture out of storage and put it into our house. The great neighbors that we had there in Richmond helped us tremendously.

Wally was lucky because Virginia Tech had two really good quarterbacks. They had a returning senior named Bob German and a junior named Don Strock. According to Wally's notes: "Remembered them from a junior varsity game which Virginia Tech had played against the University of Kentucky in Lexington." Wally said those were the two best quarterbacks he had seen on any team since he had been coaching at Kentucky.

Virginia Tech, under the previous head coach, Jerry Claiborne, was not a passing team, so after spring practice, all the sports writers in Virginia were talking about Charlie Coffey and his newfound passing attack under Wally English.

Even though it was hard to leave Richmond again, we were able to sell a house for a small profit. The boys and I headed for Southwest Virginia and Blacksburg. When you go to a new place, you are always anxious to see how you will be received and how you will like the new community. Everyone in Blacksburg was very excited about the new offensive system for the football team. The president of the university, T. Marshall Hahn, was really into athletics and wanted to fill the recently expanded Hokie Stadium. Under what the VT people perceived as an unexciting football team, the average attendance was about thirty-five thousand for each home game. Hahn said Virginia Tech wanted to fill the stadium. He was a good guy; he used to come to the football facility and play racquetball with the football coaches. He liked Wally a lot because Wally had brought a new and exciting offense to the Hokies. Also, he knew Wally was a good recruiter. This President was so much into athletics and especially football that he would call Wally at home to see how his recruiting visits had gone. It was interesting to me that as a true education person, he understood that a quality athletic program would shine a good light on the whole university and in time that would be more money for VT.

We bought a lot in a new subdivision in Blacksburg. The building inspector lived right on top of the hill only about three hundred yards from our house; his name was Pete Snyder. He and his partner had just built a lot of apartments in Blacksburg because there was relatively little university housing. Snyder's partner was Harry Hunt III. Harry Hunt's wife was Mary Ellen Hunt who still, to this day, is one of my best friends. It did not take Wally long to start construction on a new home for us in Apperson Park. Some of the boosters of VT, who wanted to see the program go, helped Wally with some house plans. Pete and Harry allowed some of their carpenters to build our house. It was a white brick house on a double lot with a mansard roof. We were happy to get moved. Wally came to pick us up in a university station wagon. He took the boys and me to the new house. The furniture followed soon after.

We had not been in the house but about two months when a man and his wife came to us and said, "We would like to buy your house."

I said, "That is very nice of you, but we've only been here a short time, and we would have to build a new house."

The lady said to me, "That's okay, we will give you time to build a new house. Ask your husband how much you want for your house."

Even though it was very unusual, Wally and I spoke about it and decided if the people would give us $65,000 for a house (remember, this was back in the old days; $65,000 was a lot of money), we would sell it to them. When the lady came back in about a week, I told her.

In the meantime, the postmaster in Blacksburg, a man named Harlan Little, owned the building lot immediately behind our house. Wally asked him if he would sell the lot. He said he would sell the lot for $10,000.

Wally said to him, "I'm in the process of selling my house."

The postmaster said, "Well, you've only been in that house for two months. Why do you want to sell it?"

Anyhow, the people bought the house, we bought the lot, and Wally started building another house that summer. It was bigger than the house we had just sold; it had two additional wings on it. This new house with a large lot gave us a park-like setting. We enjoyed Blacksburg and Virginia Tech very much. It was a great place for our young family to grow. Apperson Park in those days was a place with nice houses and large lots; many university and successful business people lived there. Our kids rode their bicycles in the street; we asked them to be home by dark, but if they were not home by dark, we really didn't worry about it. Wally ended up coaching Don Strock, who led the nation in passing in 1972. He was drafted by Miami. He played for the Dolphins for seventeen years. He eventually became Dan Marino's backup when the Dolphins had their Super Bowl teams under Don Shula.

The 1971 Virginia Tech team won only four games that season. They were four and seven. Dan Henning moved to the Houston Oilers as an assistant coach, so Charlie named Wally the offensive coordinator for the 1972 season. It was a blessing to have Dan Strock as the quarterback for the 1972 season. Wally worked really hard putting in his offense. Wally felt his pass protection was very important in his "check with me" offense.

The quarterback had to control the receivers' pass routes and the pass protection on the line of scrimmage. Charlie was not sure it would work. He questioned Wally's judgment many times during spring practices and wanted Wally to spend more time on the running game. Even in the first game, Charlie was an overbearing head coach, and many times told Wally at halftime to run the ball more and not throw so many passes. Wally felt he should call plays to the weakness of the defense.

"Check with me" was what Wally called it. Wally believed any offensive play called in the huddle was purely and simply a guess. Wally taught Dan Strock how to attack the defenses he saw on the line using the "check with me" system. Wally called the formations from the press box. Strock plugged in the appropriate play; for example, Wally's offense had plays to go against cover to cover. Charlie had no idea what was being called in the line of scrimmage. However, when the 1972 season was over, Virginia Tech led the nation in passing.

In fact, the highlight of the 1972 season was when the Hokies beat Oklahoma State in Blacksburg. Dave Strock, Dan's older brother, a left-footed kicker, kicked two 50-yard field goals to cap the victory. The overall record of 6–4–1 was Charlie Coffey's best at Virginia Tech. But at the end of the season, Charlie was fired and the whole staff was also let go. This was something "new" to our family. Welcome to coaching.

*****

One of the really nice things about Virginia Tech and Blacksburg is that the coaches were given free memberships to the city golf course and the Blacksburg Country Club. The country club had a nice place to eat and a great swimming pool for the families in the summer. Our eldest son, Jon, played a lot of golf on the city course. Jon always wanted Wally to play golf with him. He wanted to beat his dad. They usually could only play nine holes because of Wally's tight coaching schedule. One day, they were playing, and they were tied going into the ninth hole. Wally shot a 5, and Jon shot a 4.

Wally said, "I guess you get the new set of clubs, Jon."

Jon said, "Aw, that's okay, Dad. I'll just take your set of clubs."

*****

We often visited Harry and Mary Ellen Hunt in their house in Ocean Reef. If you take a look, you can see why we liked a little midwinter break to the Florida Keys each winter. Ocean Reef is seventeen miles off Key Largo in the Atlantic Ocean. It was a favorite get away for past presidents. The security is excellent, and the scenic beauty is incomparable. Wally and our family loved it. Great golf, great food, great weather, good people on the reef. My father, J. P., went there first but thought Ocean Reef was too far from Miami / Fort Lauderdale. It was just right for Harry and Mary Ellen. They first rented a house, but when a house became available to buy, they grabbed it for a little over one million. The upkeep was unbelievable. It was always something—shrubs, grass cutting, sod clean-up, tree trimming. We went there as a family every winter. The boys went fishing every year and cooked what they caught. There was a fruit stand called "Robert is Here" with the freshest and best fruits and vegetables you could find in Florida City. We loved their produce.

There was a big table and a grill on their covered patio. We ate well and told many stories about the days of old. Wally always caught a lot of heck for being too hard on our boys. Harry and Wally always told of what athletic heroes they were.

Usually, it was seventy-five degrees in Florida and freezing and snowing in Louisville. It seems we lucked out every year. Thanks, Harry and Mary Ellen. Thanks, Virginia Tech.

The University of
Nebraska: 1973

Since Wally's offense had led the nation in passing, he had several options to pursue. Wally wanted to really see what big time football was about, so he accepted a position at the University of Nebraska as an assistant coach and recruiter. In those days, that was about as big as it got. Tom Osborne had just been hired as the new head coach, one of the best coaches we ever coached under. We were low man on the totem pole.

Wally helped Tom with quarterback David Humm's passing techniques. Tom coached Humm's brain, and Wally coached his throwing mechanics. Wally also did some scouting of the opponents and a lot of recruiting. I can remember Lincoln as being a friendly city, but it was a very cold place to live. I remember one game it was so cold, I stayed in the restroom the whole game. We lived in a big old farmhouse. I can remember the deep snow and Wally having to walk to work when the temperature dropped to thirty-five degrees below zero.

After each game, the coaches would go out to eat. After my first Cornhusker game, I had never met any of the coaches. We were late getting to the restaurant. As we were going in, Coach Osborne and his wife were just leaving. They came back into the restaurant and sat with us. I doubt that was something he wanted to do because people would not leave him alone; when you are the head coach, everyone wants to talk to you or get an autograph. He did it because he was very nice, and we were the new kids on the block, and it sure made us feel good.

We went to the 1974 Cotton Bowl and won. Wally got another Bowl watch. We were only in Lincoln for one year before we went to Detroit to coach for the Lions.

Detroit Lions:
1974-1977

We got a call from Raymond Berry, whom we had coached with at Arkansas. The head coach at Detroit had died, and they needed a running back coach. Wally was director of player personnel for the new World Football League and was about to fly to California for a meeting.

Raymond said, "On your way, stop in Kansas City. Detroit is playing there. I want to recommend you for the Lions' running back coach."

Wally never made it to California. He flew back to Detroit with the team. I sent him clothes. We boxed and packed up the house and headed off to Detroit.

Off we went to what I called the "murder capital of the world." I couldn't believe that Wally wanted to take me and these four boys to Detroit, but off we went.

Wally said, "We will find a nice place in the suburbs."

The Lions put us up in a very nice hotel, provided all our meals, and gave us access to a real estate agent who helped us find a place to live. Our friends, Raymond and Sally Barry, lived in the subdivision called Beverly Hills. They helped us find a house near to them. We rented a nice house while we searched that area for a house to buy.

*****

The Lions had lost Don McCafferty to a heart attack in the summer of 1974, and Rick Forzano was promoted to Head coach. The Lions's coaching staff was offensive coordinator Raymond Berry, offensive backs Wally, defensive line Eddy Khayat (who had been a head coach for the Philadelphia Eagles), linebackers John Meyer, defensive secondary Bob Holloway (who had been a head coach for the St. Louis Cardinals), and special teams Jerry Glanville. That season, the Lions were 7–7. At the end, Rick Forzano fired John Meyer, Bob Holloway, and Eddie Khayat. There were lots of stories about those firings in the Detroit Free Press.

After every NFL season, there was always a pre-draft for all the NFL coaches in Mobile, Alabama. The players were evaluated by every team and every coach. There were always tables of good seafood, lots of good humor, and comradery between all the coaches; even the fired coaches were sent by the Lions.

Back in Detroit after the evaluation in Mobile, the new staff was getting together: offensive backs Wally, offensive line Bruce Beatty, wide receivers Raymond Berry, defensive backs Jimmy Carr, defensive line Fritz Shurmur, interior line Joe Bugel, and linebackers Jerry Glanville.

*****

We went to dinner one night to meet a player. They told us what time to meet. When we got to the restaurant, it looked very dark and strange. We thought this was a joke on Wally since he was the new coach. We pulled up. Someone came to park the car, and we went in. I noticed bullet holes in the door plus the walls.

It really was a nice restaurant. The bullet holes were from Al Capone when he came and shot up the place. The restaurant left them because they were a conversation piece.

*****

My sons loved Detroit. Our sons attended St. Regis grade school and then Brother Rice High School where Al Fracassa was the football coach. We lived in a very nice, tightly knit community that surrounded the school and church. When we first arrived in the Detroit suburb of Birmingham, our son, Jon, was to be an eighth grader, and our son, Stephen, was to be a seventh grader. Probably Birmingham was one of the nicest areas in which we have ever lived.

St. Regis grade school and Brother Rice High School were immediately adjacent to Marion High School. The house we bought was on a dead-end street that abutted Marion High School. Our sons simply had to walk across approximately one hundred yards in the rear of Marion High School, then they arrived at school. They could stay at our house until the first school bell rang, then they could hurriedly walk to school without being late.

The first day of school football practice, Wally said, "I had to have the boys in Detroit by August 1 for football practice, Mr. Byrnes." Mr. Byrnes was the head coach of the eighth-grade team, though Wally was kidding him. Wally had once told the coach of the grade school how good the boys were.

We watched practice. When it was over, I asked to speak to the coach. He came over and said, "You want me?" I explained that my husband had called him and told him about our sons. The coach laughed.

He said, "People are always calling me. I don't believe them."

This Catholic school was one of the best in Birmingham. Needless to say, both boys started, Jon as quarterback and Steve as center.

We lived in that little area around the church and the schools for four years. Our son, Jon, became the starting quarterback for Brother Rice High School. During that time, Brother Rice won twenty-five of twenty-six games and two Michigan 5-A state championships. Jon was voted the outstanding high school quarterback in America and won the Hertz Number 1 award for high school track-and-field athletes. He received many scholarship offers. He decided to attend Michigan State, where he injured his right shoulder and did not play again until he transferred to Tulane University. Jon still holds the state high jump record.

Our second son, Steve, also played for Brother Rice, and he was a starting safety as a sophomore. Steve later played quarterback at Provo High School in Utah when Wally coached at BYU. Son number three, Daniel, and number four, Thomas, both attended St. Regis grade school when we were in Detroit.

*****

We lived approximately twenty miles from downtown. The old Detroit Lions office was, at that time, immediately across the street from Tiger Stadium. Wally and Raymond would carpool to work each day. One week, Raymond would drive; the next week, Wally would drive. The Detroit Lions provided all their coaches with automobiles. The wives of the coaches were allowed to come to the Lions office to pick out the color, the interior, and the accessories that the coach's custom-built car would include. I can still remember going with Sally Berry to the Lions office to meet with the car designer. This was a man with a book of color fragments for your car's interior. He also had paint samples for your car's exterior.

As I recall, I picked out a gray station wagon with a blue vinyl top. You guessed it: the Lions' colors are blue and gray. I said yes to every option available. I said yes to all 127 pages in the guy's book, so we had this beautiful, beautiful station wagon. I was very proud of it. We took our family to church and to social gatherings in that car. After we had had it about two or three weeks, Sally and I decided to go to Birmingham to shop. You guessed it again: as I was turning the corner, someone backed into the street and collided with my beautiful car.

"No problem, Mrs. English, we will fix it good as new. However, in the meantime, you're going to have to drive this Thunderbird. Coach English won't mind you driving a sports car, will he?"

"I'm sure he won't," I said.

It took about two weeks to get my station wagon repaired. I enjoyed driving the red Thunderbird. The whole family could not get into the Thunderbird, so we had to take our other car if the family was going someplace.

*****

William Clay Ford, the owner of the Lions, had the idea that some players and coaches should go out to dinner. Wally did not take all the running backs out to dinner, but he did take Steve Owens, the fullback, and Altie Taylor out to dinner.

Steve was the highest-paid back on the team. He had cultivated a good relationship with Mr. Ford, so when it came time to take Steve out to dinner, Steve and his wife came to our house. We had a few hors d'oeuvres, then we headed to this very fancy restaurant in downtown Detroit. The idea was that the coaches could go to Mr. Ford's secretary, tell her who they were taking out to dinner, where they were going, and estimate approximately what the cost would be. She would then give them money to pay the restaurant bill. In those days, a restaurant tab for four people would probably be $100–$150. Mr. Ford's secretary told Wally, "Well, since you're taking Steve Owens at eight, you better take two hundred. Here's $200. Bring the receipt."

We got to the restaurant, had a nice meal, and the bill came: it was $250. Wally had to borrow $50 from Steve Owens. Steve said he'd get the money back from Mr. Ford, which I'm sure he did.

Then it was time to take out Altie Taylor and his wife. Altie was not so sophisticated, but his wife was. She was working on her doctorate degree. We took Altie and his wife to the Fox and Hounds restaurant, a very popular place in Birmingham, Michigan. We did the whole thing: we had the hors d'oeuvres, we had drinks, we had conversation, and then the waiter came.

The waiter said, "Are you ready to give me your order for the main course?"

Wally and I had been to the Fox and Hounds many times. We enjoyed it. They had outstanding lamb chops. Wally and I both ordered the grilled lamb chops. Altie's wife was sophisticated; she ordered a fillet.

The wife was helping him. "Would you like a nice steak, dear?"

"No."

"Would you like some fish or shrimp?"

"No."

Wally asked Altie, "Would you like some oysters?"

Altie replied, and I will never forget it, "No, I don't like anything that comes from hogs" obviously thinking of mountain oysters.

While at Detroit, all the running backs were black except for Steve Owens. Funny the things we remember. One day during the season, we were supposed to have a dinner for all the running backs. They requested chitlins, and we made them. The NFL went on strike, the dinner was canceled, and we had to throw them out. Even the dog would not eat them.

*****

It was cold in Detroit while we were there. The snow usually did not melt completely until April. It was even cold at the end of the football season. The Lions always played a game on Thanksgiving. I can remember Detroit playing Denver on Thanksgiving in 1974. It started to snow at halftime. The game was played on Thursday; it snowed Thursday, Friday, Saturday, and Sunday. We ended up with 39 inches of snow. Wally also remembers that because that was the day that Steve Owens hurt his knee. Wally and Steve had a good relationship.

*****

It was Christmastime. I was friends with Betty Forzano, Rick's wife, so I asked her what she thought would be an appropriate gift for the staff to give Rick as a Christmas present. She thought a silver-engraved tray would be nice and much appreciated. Wally carried the suggestion to the staff, and everybody said okay. So Wally was empowered to get a set of goblets. Wally went to the jewelers and had the silver set made: eight glasses and an engraved silver tray. It said, "To our leader, have a great career. From your staff," and then it listed everyone's name. I can still remember the cost, $397, or $50 each. When Wally came back with the gift, the other assistants refused to pay. Christmas week, Wally placed the gift on the meeting room table with a card that said, "Merry Christmas, Coach Forzano. From your coaching staff."

*****

The quarterback had not been there long: Gary Danielson came to the Lions as a graduate from Purdue. The Lions were loaded with quarterbacks. As fate would have it, the Lions were playing the Houston Oilers in the Astrodome. Wally was throwing passes to the running backs in warm-ups before the game. Joe Reed asked Wally, "Coach, can I throw those passes to the running backs? I don't ever get to do anything in pregame warm-up."

"Sure, Joe. Sorry, we should have you doing more," Wally said.

As the game with the Oilers started, Greg Landry hurt his knee in the first quarter, and Bill Munson was injured in the second quarter. Enter Joe Reed, the backup who never got to do anything. Joe played the rest of that game and was the

Lions starting quarterback for the remainder of the season. Gary Danielson hung in there and became the starter the next year.

*****

Wally coached under two head coaches while we were in Detroit, Rick Forzano and Tommy Hudspeth. Russ Thomas was the general manager. William Clay Ford was a good owner. He was very generous to the players and coaches. We have always driven Ford products since we left the Lions. Wally enjoyed coaching for the Lions. My sons and I enjoyed living in Birmingham, Michigan, and being associated with the Lions. Even though the Lions were great to us, we as a coaching staff did not win enough games.

Wally was sad when all were fired; he was the only coach retained by Tommy Hudspeth in 1976. Coach Hudspeth stayed as head coach with the Lions for two years; he then also was fired. Hudspeth, before coming to the Lions, had been the head coach at BYU. LaVell Edwards, who replaced Hudspeth as head coach at BYU, interviewed Wally to be the offensive coordinator for the Cougars in Provo, Utah.

Brigham Young University: 1978-79

When LaVell Edwards hired Wally as a football coach, he also had to be approved into the Mormon religious community.

LaVell said, "Okay, tomorrow we are going to Salt Lake to meet with the twelve apostles."

Wally and LaVell got into LaVell's car, and they headed for Salt Lake City. It was an hour drive on I-15 north to Salt Lake City. When they arrived at the Mormon Tabernacle, LaVell took Wally inside where they saw many Mormon scenes of Brigham Young, and finally, they came to some stairs. There was an usher at the stairs.

LaVell said to the usher, "Hello, I am LaVell Edwards, the head football coach at BYU, and this is Coach English. We are here to see the twelve apostles."

The usher said, "Okay, Coach, go right up."

At the top of the stairs was a large room. It had seventy chairs around the exterior of the room. There was a large table with twelve chairs around it with one throne chair. All were obviously for the quorum of seventy, the twelve apostles, and the profit. Wally and Coach Edwards sat and waited for a few minutes, when two members of the twelve apostles appeared and introduced themselves—one was from Michigan and the other was from Arizona. The apostle from Michigan had heard of Wally from his days with the Detroit Lions. Without delay, the apostles got right to work. They asked him if he smoked, drank, or ran around with other women. Wally responded no to all these questions. They wanted to know if Wally had any questions and if he could abide by the Mormon rules. They explained that the church had strict rules about honor and chastity: no extra women. The days of multiple wives were over, no obscene language, no drunkenness, no large consumption of pork, etc. Wally answered honestly that he could abide by these rules, as he lived by these rules of morality already.

They said, "Okay, then; you're hired."

Wally thought it was a jury. They never once asked him about football.

They drove back to Provo, and Wally started coaching as the offensive coordinator.

We were leaving Detroit. Wally was on the moving truck. The phone rang; Houston was calling, wanting him to come to Houston for an interview with the Oilers. Wally flew to Houston to interview. Our moving truck was headed to BYU; however, Wally had instructed the moving truck to stop in Nebraska. If he took the Houston job, it would head to Texas, and if he didn't, it would continue to Provo. He didn't, so Jon and Steve drove our white truck, and Tom and I drove the car. We also had to take Dan to the airport, so he could go to Germany. Then we headed to Utah.

Not long after his initial interview, Wally was to be introduced to the BYU faculty and academic community at a general assembly. When the time came, LaVell spoke and introduced Wally. There were probably ten thousand people there.

Wally, in an attempt to be funny, said, "This really is a big opportunity for a Catholic boy from Kentucky. I just came from visiting with the twelve apostles and seeing all the shrines of Joseph Smith and Brigham Young and the Tabernacle."

There was no laughter. The crowd did not perceive Wally's remarks as humorous. However, they liked him as a football coach.

That summer, Jon and Steve were going to Stanford for summer camp. Wally was going to California to recruit. Dan would fly from Germany to San Francisco where we would meet Jon and Steve from camp. Tom and I would stay in a hotel while they were at camp, and then we would all drive back together. As we drove home, we stopped at Winnemucca, Nevada. There was only one motel with one room available, so we took it. It seemed like a strange motel, but it was all we could find. About a week later, I read that the motel we stayed in had closed down because it was a hotel for prostitutes. What a place to take four boys!

Wally enjoyed coaching at BYU. LaVell Edwards and his wife, Patty, are beautiful people. LaVell allowed Wally to coach and insert his offense. BYU had some good players.

It was a little different living in Utah. As you probably know, the predominant religion in Utah is Mormonism. The LDS, Latter-Day Saints, religion is good but different from the Catholic religion. My sons and I enjoyed being on the western edge of the Rocky Mountains. It is beautiful country. Even though Jon stayed behind in Detroit, he came to Utah for Christmas. He brought home eight friends and skied every day. Robert Redford owned the ski resort in the area where BYU had begun ski classes in the 1940's, so they got to ski free because of BYU.

Provo, Utah, was a quiet little town. It is the town of Brigham Young University and a center for Mormon philosophy. The prophet—the President of the Latter-Day Saints—was in Provo almost every day. He liked interacting and speaking with the BYU students. One of his favorite examples and statements was "Lengthen your stride and quicken your pace." It was hard not to admire and respect him. He certainly was a leader, and he deserved the respect he received from his followers. However, Salt Lake City and the Mormon Tabernacle was the center; it was the headquarters.

BYU was a lot different from the hard-nosed approach which we had been exposed to at the University of Kentucky with Charlie Bradshaw and former Alabama players Charlie Pell and Leon Fuller and Coach Bob Ford. LaVell Edwards and his assistant coaches—Garth Hall, Norm Chow, Tom Ramage, and Dave Kragthorpe—were softer and not as aggressive as the Kentucky coaches. The Mormon attitude was different from the "kill or be killed" philosophy emanating from the "Bear Bryant regime." However, one of the big advantages the BYU program had was the return missionary agreement.

It is expected of each Mormon young man that he undertakes a missionary obligation. Usually, they do this sometime during their first or second year in college. The NCAA allows missionary students to resume their athletic career after completing a two-year mission. Therefore, many BYU student athletes are bigger and stronger as 23- or 24-year-old juniors and seniors than they would be if they had gone straight through college and finished at 20 or 21 years old.

Because Wally had this opportunity to coach so many good passing quarterbacks, I once asked him what the difference was. Why were his quarterbacks always good? What made them better? His answer was simple: pass protection. He said because the BYU offensive linemen had two extra years to grow and mature on their missions, they were bigger and stronger and became better pass protectors. That was a contributing factor to the Cougars having so many good, successful quarterbacks. LaVell pretty much gave Wally a free hand in controlling the BYU offense. Dave Kragthorpe, Garth Hall, and Norm Chow allowed Wally to implement some new ideas that he brought from the

Detroit Lions. They all fit in pretty well since Tommy Hudspeth, the Lions' head coach, had come from BYU.

When Wally arrived at BYU, there were some strange things going on. LaVell was allowing two of the Osmond brothers to go through the quarterback warm-up drills with the BYU quarterbacks. It took two or three weeks for Wally to convince LaVell to ask the Osmond brothers to leave the practice sessions. Wally had a hard time convincing LaVell to be completely serious about practice. Another problem was the golf team hitting balls on the football field while the football team was practicing. Wally wanted total concentration during practice. LaVell was too nice and too easy to get along with. It took some time to gain control of the practice situation. It, however, paid dividends, as BYU won the Western Athletic Conference [WAC] championship at the earliest date in conference history.

Wally coached Jim McMahon and Marc Wilson to be one of the best offenses in BYU history. Jim McMahon was a first team all conference quarterback, and Marc Wilson was the second team quarterback; they both were first-round NFL picks. Michael Chronister was a first team wide receiver, and Lloyd Jones was a second team all conference wide receiver. The offensive line was mostly made up of return missionaries. They afforded McMahon and Wilson good pass protection so that BYU had an excellent pass offense. LaVell said it was the earliest in the season the Cougars had clinched the WAC championship and gotten a bowl bid.

The Cougars were to play the Navy in the Fiesta Bowl in San Diego. It was a really nice event. The whole family got to spend a week in the San Diego sun. There were lots of festivities and social events. It was almost like the game was secondary; it was fun. BYU won and returned to Provo to prepare for a visit to the Japan Bowl to play against the University of Nevada, Las Vegas. Our whole family traveled with the team to Tokyo and spent a week there in the Princess Hotel. I remember one day I missed Jon and Steve and found them to be in Jim McMahon's room playing cards. McMahon had a bathtub full of sake. Wally still talks about the press box arrangements in the Japanese stadiums. The Japan Bowl was played in a baseball stadium; there was no press box to call the plays from. Wally had to call the plays from a section of box seats in the front row of the baseball stadium. He can still remember the Japanese fans hanging over the rails of the box seats, listening to every word he was speaking. BYU won, and we returned to Provo.

Wally liked to tell some stories on Jim McMahon, who he felt was a little different from most of the other quarterbacks he coached. One evening after a spring practice, the team had just finished the training table dinner. The coaches had gone home, and most of the players had gone to their study sessions. Wally had not been home long when he received a call from one of the offensive linemen. I could overhear the young man speaking to Wally about something he perceived as being serious.

He said, "Coach, you better come back over here."

"What's wrong?" Wally asked.

"McMahon's acting crazy, Coach!"

"Well, what's he doing?" Wally demanded.

"You better get over here and see for yourself!" the young man said.

BYU has two twin tower dormitories, one for the male students and one for the female students. These dormitories have what amounts to a concrete patio in front of and between the two buildings. Wally said when he arrived, Jim McMahon was sitting on a bench drinking something. Wally said McMahon was saying something derogatory about one of the church founders.

Wally, along with two offensive linemen, approached McMahon and said, "Okay, guys, take him to his room." Wally stayed around for a little while and tried to smooth things over. He recovered the bottle from which McMahon was drinking, where-upon McMahon, from his dormitory room, screamed out, "Wally! Wally! Give me back my bottle!"

Wally told him, "I'm going to give this bottle to Coach Edwards. You can get it back from him." That's the last we heard about the bottle.

McMahon was a good athlete but something of a character. He was always acting the fool, and he was always carrying out pranks. When they had the quarterback meetings at 2:30, he would wait until 2:28 to report to duty and then have some sort of excuse for why he was not there earlier. He was always there but never earlier.

He got into the first game and ran for a touchdown on a play where he should not have gotten the ball. He was a king at what should not have been his expression. LaVell could not have been more disenchanted with him. LaVell liked Marc Wilson better but allowed Wally to play the quarterback of his choice.

McMahon was better than Wilson as a street player. Wilson was a better quarterback from a pure quarterback standpoint. Once LaVell had the parents come to see who the starter should be. Wally told them that Jim McMahon was the better player, and that shut them up for a while until Marc Wilson had a really good game against some team. He passed for over three hundred yards and ran for over one hundred. He was the back of the week and proud of it. Wilson started the next game and was the big guy versus Wyoming, who had not had a touchdown pass thrown against them. McMahon threw three touchdown passes, though, and ran for one against them and won the game, 49–3. It was certainly a battle for who was the best.

Marc Wilson's story rarely got told. Marc Wilson was 6'5" and every bit as good as McMahon. However, he was never mentioned in the same breath as McMahon. Marc Wilson was never as flamboyant as McMahon. Wilson could pass as good as McMahon, but he was never given credit for it. He was just as good a quarterback. Wilson always had to take to being second while McMahon was around because even the coaches didn't recognize his talent.

Wally was very fortunate to have the opportunity to coach two first-round draft choices in Jim McMahon and Marc Wilson at BYU. At BYU's bowl game, Joe Pendry from University of Pittsburg saw Wally's offense. He called the head coach at the University of Pittsburgh to tell him to hire Wally to replace Jimmy Johnson. We lucked out again when Coach Jackie Sherrill asked Wally to come to the University of Pittsburgh as offensive coordinator. When Coach Sherrill called, he told Wally that Pitt had a good team returning and would probably be favored in every game the upcoming season. Even though we loved Provo and BYU, he would be getting a pay raise, and Pitt was a top-notch program in the east and played a tough national schedule. Wally submitted his resignation to LaVell, and we headed from Utah to Pennsylvania. Wally flew on to Pittsburgh, and I and the boys drove our old Mercedes cross-country.

The University of Pittsburgh

1979-80

One of our favorite places of all the nine colleges and three professional teams where we coached had to be the University of Pittsburgh. Jackie Sherrill was a defensive coach and allowed Wally to coach the offense. He allowed Wally to install the system, give assignments to the offensive assistant coaches, and call the plays on game days.

Wally felt that Pitt had excellent players and coaches in the old days when John Majors was the head coach at Pitt. The school, which had been a real powerhouse in years gone by, was ready for a reawakening. When scholarships were unlimited, Majors gave seventy-six freshman football scholarships to his first team. That team with Tony Dorsett as a running back four years later won the national championship in 1976. A lot of good players were encouraged to come to Pitt after they won that national championship. Even though Pitt had good coaches and good players, the facilities were not outstanding. The University of Pittsburgh's stadium was old, dating back to the early 1900s. There was no indoor facility. The practice facilities were not good either. The team, both the offense and the defense, had to practice on the game field. If it rained, the team went inside to watch a film and had to walk through the weight room.

One day, after a spring practice session in which the players and coaches were driven inside by poor weather conditions, Wally was frustrated. He found the head groundskeeper, a man named Bo. Wally asked Bo if there was a place where they could practice inside.

Wally just told Bo, "To avoid all the problems, don't tell anybody; just get these cages out of here."

What became "the dungeon" at Pitt was created by Bo and his crew removing the Jonas Salk's polio vaccine monkey cages from the old basketball facility, disposing of them, mopping the floor with disinfectant, and thereby giving Pitt an indoor facility. After that, every time it rained and even some other times, the offensive team would go into "the dungeon" for some workouts. By Wally doing this, Coach Sherrill was never in any danger of being viewed as someone who created controversy.

When we were in Pittsburgh, it was before these latter-day cleanup campaigns had modernized the old steel town to a vibrant city. We loved the ethnic areas of Pittsburgh. The old strip district was where you could find all sorts of ethnic food and customs, mostly Italian.

We first rented a house in a Pittsburgh suburb called Oakmont, then we rented another house before building our own house. There was a banker named Bill Bier who had some vacant land north of Pittsburgh on the way to Butler, Pennsylvania. Mr. Bier was willing to sell the land at a reasonable price. We bought the land, and Wally again built us a nice house.

The reason that Pittsburgh was a great place for our family was because of the very nice people who lived there. Joe Massaro, who owned a construction company, and his wife were really nice people. Joe lived in Oakmont, a northern suburb of Pittsburgh. There was a famous golf course there at the Oakmont Country Club. Joe owned six acres in a prominent place which adjoined the Oakmont Country Club golf course. The country club would have gatherings for Jackie Sherrill and the University of Pittsburgh assistant football coaches. Once when Wally and I were at the Massaro's for a cookout and playing a little boccie, I asked Mrs. Massaro, "Why don't you all come to the country club for some of the Pitt functions?"

She told me, "We are not welcome at Oakmont because we are Italian."

Wally and I did not realize that and felt bad for the Massaros. She then said, "Don't worry, because Joe is making arrangements to buy the Oakmont Country Club!"

After we had traveled around the country, we saw Joe Massaro signs posted in front of many building sites all over the eastern United States. He built schools, churches, office buildings, and many municipal buildings everywhere. It really was a shame that the Oakmont Country Club would not let them join because of their nationality.

*****

We went to a bowl game every year, so wives and families got to go. The games were usually around Christmas, so when we would arrive at our hotel, there would be a tree in our room and presents for the boys. We were invited to a high society ball—some of the guests included Merv Griffin and Zsa Zsa Gabor, to name a few. The ladies I knew that were going ordered these gowns from New York and Paris. I certainly could not afford that, so I found a consignment shop outside of Pittsburgh and bought the prettiest red gown I have ever had. It still had the original price tag on it; I paid $30. The dress was the hit of the party: even Zsa Zsa commented on it.

Each school takes the wives to one away game. While at Pittsburgh, the wives got to go to the Army game. The wives got to stay in New York City, all expenses paid, and we were even given money to spend, all because I traveled with the coach.

*****

We stayed at the University of Pittsburgh for three years. Pitt played in three bowl games and won them all. At the end of our time there, Pitt was ranked sixth in the nation and had been ranked second before losing a game to Florida State in Tallahassee. Wally had been offered some other assistant coaching jobs but wanted to stay in Pittsburgh because he felt they were the best players he had the chance to coach.

Wally said several times to me, "Peggy, you don't just run across players like this all on the same team very often."

That was verified when Mark May, Jimbo Covert, and Russ Grimm were all taken in the first round of the NFL draft from Pitt's offensive line. Randy McMillan, the Pitt fullback, was also taken in the first round. Dan Marino was drafted as well. This was only on the offensive side of the ball. The defense had many of their players also drafted in the first round. I was not as familiar with the defensive players, but I do know that the entire Pitt second string was drafted, and Ricky Jackson was a long-time outstanding linebacker for the New Orleans Saints. Hugh Green was second choice for the Heisman trophy his senior year. He later played for the Miami Dolphins in the NFL. Wally told me those had to be the best college players on one team that he was ever associated with.

RICK TROCANO AND DAN MARINO

When Wally got to Pittsburgh, there was a junior to be quarterback. His name was Rick Trocano. He had been the starting quarterback as a sophomore. The Panthers had been a running team. They had run The Veer. Wally's offense incorporated a lot more passing. When Dan Marino arrived as a freshman, it was a battle at quarterback to see if Trocano or Marino would be the starter.

Finally, as the 1979 season began, Wally and the staff decided that Rick Trocano was the starter because of his experience. He had been the starter for a year as a sophomore. Trocano was an all-around player. He was from Brooklyn High School in Brooklyn, Ohio. Marino, however, was not far behind. Jackie Sherrill had promised Mr. Marino, Dan's father, when he was recruiting Danny that if Marino came to Pittsburgh, he would be the starter as a freshman.

Trocano started the first three games. In the fourth game versus the Navy, Trocano got to run out of the pocket on a pass play. Then Marino went into the game. He threw two touchdown passes and was the starter for the rest of the season. Coach Sherrill said to Wally, "Trocano is too good to sit on the bench behind Marino."

"We are going to move him to safety," said Wally, so Trocano became the starting safety.

Now Marino, as a young freshman quarterback, became a little lackadaisical with not much attention to detail. He was carrying out his fakes. He was not doing the little things that it takes to be an outstanding quarterback. Finally, Wally was tired of it when Marino just refused to do what Wally was asking him to do.

One day, in the middle of practice, with no warning, Wally yelled down to Jackie Sherrill, "Coach! Send me Trocano!"

Jackie yelled to Trocano who was playing safety, "Ricky, go to Coach English."

Wally got Trocano and said, "Get in there, Ricky."

He put Marino in the back. Danny did not take a snap for three days. After Marino was willing to listen, that was what made Jackie Sherrill understand what it took to discipline a player. Wally thought Jackie had learned that from Coach Bear Bryant. From then on, Marino was willing to do all the things. Trocano stayed on offense the rest of the season and was voted outstanding player in the Gator Bowl.

After his senior season, Ricky Trocano was drafted by the Pittsburgh Steelers in the eleventh round. He played defensive back for two seasons. He also played for the Cleveland Browns. He played quarterback on one of the best Pittsburgh teams in history.

Dan Marino was the best quarterback Wally ever coached. He was big enough, fast enough, and good enough to play for anybody. We could beat just about anybody with him as our quarterback. We won thirty-three games and lost only two that season; one being to North Carolina 14–7 and one to Florida State 14–7. They were both good games that went down to the wire where it could have gone either way for either team. Unfortunately, we didn't win. Danny made the other quarterbacks look bad, like West Virginia, Penn State, South Carolina, and Florida State. He was just a superior quarterback, a great player. He made the other teams' defense look bad too. He could play like nobody else could play. He truly was the best that Wally has ever coached.

At the beginning of his junior year, Danny thought he was a great player. Jackie took away his competition: Rick Trocano was the only player that Marino feared. Jackie took Trocano away. Now, Marino had no one to fear. He was in practice "the big man": he would not carry out his jobs, he would not throw passes with authority, and he would not fear anyone taking his job away from him. He would just play around without fear of becoming second string. He played well until his last two games when Ricky was put in in place of Marino. Ricky played most of the Bowl game and was voted player of the game.

*****

After Pittsburgh beat Penn State two years in a row, Joe Paterno, the head coach at Penn State, called Wally to come for an interview. Jackie Sherrill said, "If you go for the interview, you better get the job because you won't have one here."

Miami Dolphins: 1981-82

Even though we dearly loved the University of Pittsburgh and the great boosters of Western Pennsylvania, the time came to move on. Our next stop was the Miami Dolphins. Miami was the big time. Don Shula was a big-time coach. Wally had just been "small potatoes" until he was picked up by big Don Shula and the Miami Dolphins. Wally took the offensive coordinator job for the Dolphins and went on ahead to Miami. I was in Pittsburgh with our sons trying to get ready to move and trying to sell our house.

I stayed behind with Steve, Dan, and Tom while Wally went on to Miami. That house that we had built was twenty miles outside of Pittsburgh on Route 8 before you got to Butler. I was pregnant with our fifth child and had to drive Tommy to school every morning. It was getting close to the time for the baby to come. Steve, our second son, was a senior at Central Catholic High School in Pittsburgh. Steve had been the backup quarterback to Dan Marino, who also played football at Central Catholic High School. Steve was preparing to graduate, and Dan was a freshman quarterback at Central Catholic. They had a good coach there; his name was Rich Erdelyi, and he had also coached Dan Marino.

There had not been many babies born to the Dolphins staff in years. When my time came to deliver Andrew, our fifth son, Coach Shula gave Wally the option of picking one of two dates on which Andrew could be delivered. He allowed Wally to fly home, see the birth, and return to practice. Shula's wife, Dorothy, could relate to me well and later told me, "If I died during the football season, Don would have me frozen and then bury me after the playoffs."

When John Sandusky's wife died during the season, only he was allowed to go to the funeral. All the other assistant coaches worked that day. The NFL is big business, and Coach Shula was not about to allow any advantages to slip away.

We were doing everything we could to get ready for the move to Miami. After Andrew was born, my mother and Mary Ellen Hunt and friends came from Blacksburg to help with everything. Finally, the day came for us to move. The movers came and packed all our possessions in the boxes and put them into storage because we had no place to take them in Miami. The boys and I moved into a furnished apartment, which Wally had shared with some Miami Dolphins administrative personnel. Bob Brodhead was the assistant general manager of the Dolphins. He was moving into his new home as we were moving into the apartment, so for about a week, Bob and his son, Jason, were there. Bob's wife, Kay, was in Boca Raton getting everything ready for them to move into that house. That was a hectic week, but we got through it. Bob Brodhead would enter our life again later.

After Brodhead and the other gentlemen moved out of the apartment, Wally, Dan, Tom, Andrew, and I made the best of it until the house that Wally had built for us was completed. It was a nice house on a cul-de-sac about a thirty-minute drive from the football office. There are no basements in South Florida, so we had a lot of furniture that we could not fit into the Florida house. A few last-minute details did not materialize properly, so we had about a week from the time we had to move out of the apartment until the time we could get into our new house. Earl Morrall, one of the former Miami Dolphin quarterbacks, and his wife, Jane, were going on vacation and offered the use of their house while we were waiting to get into our house. The Morrall house was spacious and unique. It had five bedrooms all surrounding a swimming pool in the middle of the house. You could literally go from your bedroom into the swimming pool with no effort. Just before our house was completed, we moved out of the Morrall house and into a room in the Dolphins' training camp. Wally made our son, Andrew, a bed on rocker legs.

One day, the phone in our room rang, and it was Dorothy Shula on the line; she called me to welcome me to Miami. I told her how excited I was. I loved Florida. She laughed and said, "You will have lots of hot weather and lots of company." She was right.

She said, "Peggy, I'm nearby and wanted to come by and meet you." When she arrived in a floral print muumuu, I mistook her for the cleaning lady. It was very embarrassing. I opened the door and said, "We will be out shortly, and then you can come in."

"No, I'm Dorothy Shula," she said. "Don thinks a lot of your husband, Wally. He says that Wally has a sharp football mind."

Dorothy Shula and I became friends. She had five children, two boys and three girls. Both David and Michael were football coaches. David became the head coach of the Cincinnati Bengals, and Michael became the head coach at the University of Alabama. David eventually got out of coaching and got into the restaurant business. Michael went on to be an assistant coach in the NFL. The two daughters were not talked about that much. Dorothy died in 1991 from breast cancer. Don later remarried.

Finally, our house was complete, except for the air conditioning. We had to spend two nights as I recall without air conditioning. The mosquitoes were bad because the house was on a lot which backed up to the canal. We got through all the turmoil and really enjoyed living there. We stayed there for two years.

*****

Don Shula attended John Carroll University. He and Carl Taseff were the running backs for the Lobos. He played with the Baltimore Colts and the Washington Redskins. Don later became a defensive coach, coaching the defensive backs at the University of Kentucky for Blanton Collier.

Shula became an assistant at Baltimore, then became the head coach. He had John Unitas as quarterback, Raymond Berry as wide receiver, Lenny Moore as running back, and a very strong defense anchored by defensive end Gino Marchetti. Shula had a winning record and led the Colts to two Super Bowl victories before being hired by Joe Robbie to head the Miami Dolphins. Earl Morrall had been a backup quarterback for the Colts and then the Dolphins. Earl and his wife, Jane, became our friends. Jane Morrall sold clothes and became my first close friend in Miami.

Wally was the youngest coach on the Miami Dolphins coaching staff. Bill Arnsparger was the defensive coordinator, John Sandusky was the offensive line coach, Mike Scarry was the linebacker coach, and Carl Taseff was the running back coach. They had all been with Don Shula for many years. Many had been assistant coaches with him when he coached the Baltimore Colts. It was a strange setup in Miami. The administrative offices were in Joe Robbie Stadium, and the football offices were in a school on Seventeenth Street called Saint Thomas University.

The first year at Miami, Coach Shula told Wally to get a good quarterback. Wally did not hesitate and said, "Dan Marino." Dan knew Wally's offense. Wally also recommended Mark Duper. The scouts for the Dolphins said they had never heard of him and that Danny Marino had a bad senior year. Wally persisted and stood his ground. He wanted them both, so they were both drafted. Shula told Wally that he had better be right.

The first day of minicamp, Duper was awful. Shula was not happy. However, after a little coaching, Duper and Marino became known as the "dynamic duo."

"You got me two times when I was unaware," Shula said. "Being gone could not get me the third time." He said, "We are not going to throw the ball down the middle like that."

He didn't want to throw the ball and it be up for grabs like that, so Dan had to throw it to a secondary receiver. Wally can still remember playing against the Dallas Cowboys and passing for four hundred yards. Shula was surprised when we were on the board, then he saw the statistics and asked, "How many yards did we pass for?"

Someone replied, "Four hundred six yards."

He asked, "How many?"

Again, they replied, "Four hundred six."

"That is a lot," he said.

The Dolphins had the best year they had in years, and Shula and two of the players went to the 1982 Pro Bowl.

The next season, Miami had the best season they had in a long time. We made the playoffs, then we were on our way to the Super Bowl.

*****

When Wally played quarterback for the Louisville Raiders in the old United Football League, which was the predecessor of the American Football League, Bob Brodhead played for the Cleveland Bulldogs. Wally and Bob became good friends. After our first year with the Dolphins, Brodhead left to become the athletic director at Louisiana State University. Not long after

Brodhead left, he contacted Wally with the proposition that Wally would be the new head coach at LSU. Jerry Stovall, an outstanding former LSU player, was the head coach in Baton Rouge. LSU under Stovall was not super successful as the LSU people wanted. Brodhead flew to Miami, took Wally and me out to dinner, and said that the next time we ate together, we would be eating crawfish in Baton Rouge and Wally would be the new head football coach at LSU. It didn't quite work out that way. Stovall was too strong. He had too many big boosters backing him instead of Wally for the head coach position.

Don Shula was a good man who, when he was coaching, went to Catholic Mass every morning. Before Wally got the Tulane coaching job, Don came to Wally's office. He called Tulane and gave Wally a glowing recommendation. Wally said that you had to respect Don because of all the good things he did for people. However, it was best not getting on his bad side. Wally learned a lot from Don.

Tulane University:
1983-84

W e got a call to interview for the head coaching jobs at Tulane and Iowa State. The athletic director came to our house and spent five hours convincing Wally to take the Tulane job. We were promised a house, scholarships for our sons, and $70,000, which seemed like a fortune since we only made $32,000 at Miami. We were told many things that did not turn out to be true.

Wally took the Tulane job. Tulane was the graveyard of coaching. Not much of what the athletic director had told us was true.

*****

Who was recruited and signed with the University of Alabama before deciding to play professional baseball? The young man's name was Bubby Brister. If you followed football at that time, you would remember that our son, Jon, and Bubby Brister competed for the starting quarterback position at Tulane. Wally, as not to be seen as someone who was taking matters into his own hands, went to see Dr. Kelly, the president of Tulane. Wally explained the entire scenario about Jon's eligibility issues in changing schools. Dr. Kelly said that if Ralph Peterson said that Jon was eligible, then it's his call. Wally told Dr. Kelly that the athletic director, Hindman Wall, had called the NCAA and told them that the school was against our son playing. Hindman continued by saying that if we allowed this coach's son to play without sitting out a year, then it would open a new can of worms. Dr. Kelly again reassured Wally and told him that it was his call and that he was the coach, and he needed to do what he thought best for our son and for Tulane.

The first game was against Mississippi State in Starkville, Mississippi. Bubby Brister started the game at quarterback. At the end of the first half, Tulane had not scored and had not played well offensively either. Wally put Jon in as quarterback in the second half. The offense picked up, and Tulane scored two touchdowns. We still lost. In practice the next week, Jon became the starting quarterback, and all hell broke loose.

There were two attorneys who wanted to represent me and Jon. They called and said that this was total BS: the NCAA was completely off base here. They wanted our permission to sue the NCAA on behalf of Jon and me. They were going to keep Wally out of the lawsuit. Jon and I went and met with them. I can still remember they said they were going to bring the NCAA to its knees. Through lots of manipulation through the university, and with Dr. Kelly now siding with the NCAA, the lawsuit garnered headlines on the front pages and sports pages throughout the United States. Coaches were calling Wally from all over the country and asking how he got his son eligible. The media attention was incredible. I was in the Superdome one day and counted seventeen TV cameras filming Tulane's practice. The *Times-Picayune* was full of stories supporting and condemning Wally and Jon.

The next game that Tulane was to play was against Kentucky in Lexington. Jerry Claiborne was the Kentucky coach. Claiborne was quoted in an article in the *Lexington Herald-Leader* saying that he was "scared to death of Tulane's passing attack." Unfortunately, Jon hurt his wrist in the first half. Tulane lost, but it was a close game. The season dragged on. Jon had a temporary restraining order that allowed him to play through the first six games. Bubby Brister quit the team and went back to Shreveport where he played at Northeastern Louisiana without sitting out a year. So the first season at Tulane was very interesting. Hindman Wall continued his assault on Wally, his staff, and the football. Recruiting was not good. The Tulane boosters were divided. It was not fun.

*****

Living in New Orleans, however, was fun. Wally had a radio show on WWL 87—50,000 clear channel watts. Bob Brodhead, the athletic director at LSU, had had some sort of spat with WWL, who had carried the LSU football games for many years. WWL came to Wally and asked if he would like to have a radio show on their station. Tulane was a very interesting study in college sports at the time. Wally sold twenty-five one-minute radio spots to sponsors who were interested in helping him with Tulane football. Those twenty-five spots sold for $10,000 each, totaling $250,000. The cost to Wally for the time on WWL was an hour and a half each Tuesday evening from seven o'clock until eight thirty. Wally's sales pitch to the sponsors was something like, "I just want a little money from you, just enough to pay for the airtime." I can't remember exactly, but the rest of the deal was done as a trade-out. This meant that we could go to any restaurant in New Orleans for free. We could travel to anyplace, even Europe, for free; we could get rental cars, hotel rooms, groceries, flowers, and even building materials. Many of these things Wally used to upgrade the faltering Tulane football program.

At the end of the second year, because of not winning enough games under the aforementioned trying circumstances, Hindman Wall convinced Dr. Kelly to fire Wally. As soon as it was announced about Wally's termination, the Tulane administration immediately swung into action and convinced all the boosters that the sponsorship deals they had with Wally were really sponsorships for Tulane, even though Wally had signed contracts from each of those sponsors. The very elaborate contract that Hindman Wall had brought to Miami when he lured Wally away from the Miami Dolphins was never finalized. It was written up, but then the Tulane lawyers said it had to be rewritten in Napoleonic law, which is the law in Louisiana. Napoleonic law is not honored in any other state in the United States besides Louisiana. From the very beginning, when Wally discovered all the abnormalities in the Tulane athletic budget, Hindman Wall was against finalizing Wally's contract.

THINGS I GOT TO DO BECAUSE I WAS A COACH'S WIFE

Tulane was the most fun place we have lived except for Italy. Wally was the head coach, so we were invited to everything. We had a wonderful house in the French Quarter, and we were lucky enough to find a live-in maid thanks to Barbara Brennan; she knew the lady, and the lady needed a home.

Would I ever advise Wally not to take the contract to be the head football coach at Tulane University? Most definitely I would advise him not to go there, even though we had a lot of fun socially. On one particular occasion, the Dallas Cowboys invited us to a weekend of entertainment and meetings. One of Tulane's boosters told us to go to a certain exclusive restaurant in Dallas and to go to the back door and give them his name. We went to the restaurant, and there was a long line at the front door. In the line there was a very prominent big school's head coach's wife. I told Wally that if she couldn't get in, how were we going to get in? We went to the back door as we were told to do and were let in. Coming out of the back door as we were going in was the head coach, whose wife was in the line out front. He was with another woman.

We went to every Mardi Gras ball only because of Wally's position. Some of the balls are only for the Old Guard, but we got to go. We went to a birthday party on a streetcar with a jazz band, drinks, and a waiter. We went to an adult Halloween Party. The house was so big you could walk in and out of the open windows. Everyone was in costume. The winning costume was a pair of dice; the runner-up was a pregnant lady whose sign read, *I didn't know the gun was loaded.*

We could go to any restaurant and be seated immediately. Wally had trade-outs for his radio show and TV show; one was with Delta Airlines, so we took the whole family to Europe. A funny thing I remember: we had reservations made ahead of time at the hotels. We pulled up to the back of a hotel—we didn't know it was the back—and Wally took one look and said, "We are not staying here. It is not nice enough."

We then pulled around front. People were coming out in tuxes and dresses, very nice. Wally then said to all of us, "We aren't dressed nice enough."

We all laughed.

While in Europe, we bought three cars: there was not a euro then, and the dollar was very high. One of Tulane's boosters said, "Drive the cars to Amsterdam, and my shipping lines will bring them back to New Orleans."

My favorite story: we were invited to then-governor Edwin Edward's roast. I had borrowed a dress from a friend. It was very low-cut for my taste, so I kept my coat over my shoulders. When I was introduced to Governor Edwards, he noticed my very low-cut bodice. He was very charming; the next day, I received a dozen roses from him.

THE BACCHUS PARADE

It was a big deal and certainly an honor: the businessmen of New Orleans, every year, have a parade called Bacchus. It is the biggest and best parade of the celebration of Mardi Gras. There are always local people and invited guests. The King of Bacchus was Charlton Heston. Invited celebrities included the George H. W. Bush family before he became the forty-first president of the United States.

Wally rode a horse and was depicted as the captain of the guards for King Bacchus, who rode in a horse-drawn carriage with mounted guards in front and behind. Just so we encountered no horse problems, I asked Kenny Bowls, a young graduate assistant, to come to the parade and hold the horse's reins. To add to the confusion, it was the night of Wally's weekly radio show, so they did the show from his horse.

I don't know if you have ever been in New Orleans for Mardi Gras, but the Crescent City citizens are wild! They crowd the streets and push in on the parade. Wally was on the horse, and people were tugging at his boots and pant legs, screaming "Throw me something, mister!" Wally was throwing beads while he was taking calls from the radio listeners. It was crazy.

The Bacchus Parade lasted about one hour. About a quarter of the parade had gone by when Kenny Bowls excused himself to do something he had scheduled, so Wally was left on the horse with no control. He finished throwing the beads to the crowd and then finished the radio show. He was just trying to control the ole gray mare at this point. Finally, Charlton Heston's carriage turned into the hotel, and the horse was free to gallop back to the barn at the end of Canal Street. Wally had no control. He galloped fast down Canal Street and into the barn.

Wally's costume had one of those centurion helmets with the brush down the center. After all the bouncing down Canal Street, the helmet had turned sideways.

THE MAFIA CONNECTION

When you go to a new place, there are always a lot of people who want to meet you. Tulane was no different. A booster sent Wally a Mercedes Benz sports car to drive. The booster thought it would help recruiting. A former player from Tulane, and now a big concrete producer, came into Wally's office one day. He was a big, overweight man with wrinkled clothes. He was loud and boastful. He walked directly in front of Wally's desk and said, "I'm Jay Ditta. I played here, and I want to win. I'm tired of losing." He pulled out a roll of $100 bills, slammed them on Wally's desk, and said, "If this is what it takes to win, I've got plenty of it."

That made Wally uncomfortable. He said, "Please, Jay, we can't do that."

However, Jay was persistent. The next week, Jay reappeared with a trailer full of clothes: suits, sport coats, pants, sweaters, shirts, and shoes. He said to Wally, "Where can we put this stuff? I want to donate it to the program. We can give it to the most valuable player every week."

"Thank you, Jay, but we cannot do that," Wally repeated.

Jay rented a little building near the campus where he stored the things. He continued to be persistent. He kept coming to Wally's office. Soon, they became friends. Jay donated money to Wally's needs. Jay and his wife, Rose, took both Wally and I out to eat at the finest and fanciest restaurants in New Orleans. No place was too grand. The Dittas had us to their home for dinner. Jay had a special cook who made Italian pasta dishes. They had a marble table from Capri, Italy, that was so big it had to be lowered through the roof by a crane when the house was being built. Wally told me that he thought Jay was in the Mafia, but he had no proof.

As you may or may not know, the Italian Mafia has some strong religious connections. St. Joseph's Day is a big feast day for the Mafia. Jay called Wally on the phone and said that he wanted to take us out to a special celebration. He came in his big Mercedes Benz and picked us up and took us to a Gambino family picnic at the home of Carter Gambino, a mob boss in New Orleans. I remember we stayed outside at a table under a tree, afraid to join the crowd inside the house.

Not long after the Gambino party, Wally was having coffee with Jay at the Morning Call, a favorite spot of Jay's. Suddenly, Jay became very stiff and quiet, then he jumped up and ran out of the coffee shop. He came back in after a few minutes and said, "Thank God! They got it stopped." He had seen one of his concrete trucks rolling down the street with no driver. They pushed a garbage wagon in front of it. Surely, it was an act of the Mafia.

When Wally and I moved back to Louisville, we had not had any contact with people in Louisiana for about a year. The Super Bowl was to be played in New Orleans. Wally called the Jay Ditta concrete business. Lil, Jay's sister, answered.

Wally said, "Hello, Lil, can I speak to Jay?"

Lil said, "Wally, didn't you get the message I sent to you? Jay's dead."

"What!" Wally said in disbelief. "I did not get any message."

"He had a heart attack. Rose died too, same thing. Here, talk to Joey," Lil said and then handed off the phone.

"Hello, Coach," said Joey.

"Joey, we are coming to New Orleans for the Super Bowl and need a place to stay."

"You can stay in my apartment," said Joey. "It's on Louis XIV, close to your old house."

"Sorry, Joey; I didn't know about Jay."

"It's okay, Coach. Call me. I'll meet you."

So we met Joey and stayed in his apartment. Jay and Rose were gone. Mafia related, you would have to believe.

Honolulu, Hawaii: 1997-98

Wally had known Fred von Appen for a long time. Fred was on the staff at Virginia Tech when we had coached there under Charlie Coffey. When Wally coached for the Miami Dolphins, Fred was on Bill Walsh's staff for the San Francisco 49ers. When Fred was with us in Blacksburg, he was married to Sally, but now Sally was gone, and Fred had a new wife named Thea and had taken the head coaching job at University of Hawaii.

Fred wanted Wally to put in his offense for the Rainbow Warriors. Fred assured Wally that he would have full control over the offense.

Wally and Andrew drove to Los Angeles where they put our Volvo car onto the ferry to Honolulu, and then they caught a plane headed for what Fred called "Paradise." The football fortunes of the University of Hawaii had not been great. In fact, they had lost more games than they had won. Wally and Andrew were given a room in a fancy hotel in Honolulu. The room and all the food were provided. I came to Honolulu to look for a house. Andrew and I found a beautiful house in a walled neighborhood. The house had a pool and a privacy fence. It was totally furnished, and it was in our price range, so we rented it.

Andrew and I went to the store and bought towels and sheets and a big screen TV.

Hawaii was a little different from any place where we had coached before. The team practiced early in the morning before class and then had a short meeting at four o'clock each day. Wally was usually finished by five o'clock and free to come home. As you know, most teams here on the mainland in the US practice after class, and many times, Wally was not finished or free to come home until 10:00 p.m. or later. So in a way, this new schedule was a real treat because we had hours like regular people. There were many fabulous restaurants in Honolulu. Thanks to our new schedule, we could even go out to dinner as a family.

Honolulu truly was a beautiful place to live. The university had some trade-out agreements; Fred was a good guy and willing to share the trade-outs with the assistant coaches. I don't know how much you know about Hawaii, but when the Japanese economy was very strong, many Japanese people moved to the islands. They bought and built many nice houses near Honolulu. Then, as you may recall, the Japanese economy slipped, and some of those Japanese residents in Honolulu were forced to sell the elaborate homes for less than they were worth. Sometimes, they even rented out those houses. We were fortunate enough to find a beautiful house in a gated community right on a golf course, which was about 1,000 yards from the ocean. The house was completely furnished with beautiful furniture. It also had a swimming pool with a very high privacy fence around it. We were really lucky. Since Wally was finished with work early every day, he and I could walk around the golf course. It cost a lot of money to play golf on that course. The greens fees were $85.00, and the cart cost was $35.00. It is not the mentality of the native people there to spend a lot of time looking for golf balls. Each time we would walk around the golf course, we could find a lot of golf balls. It was beautiful; usually we could find twelve to fifteen golf balls each evening. We cleaned them, put them in boxes, and sent them back to our sons in Kentucky.

The Rainbow Warriors had a lot of boosters, many of whom are very wealthy. We were invited to lots of luaus and many boat trips. It seemed that everybody had a boat. We would catch fish, and they would clean it right on the boat, so we learned to eat raw fish. Wally and Fred went to a lot of clinics on the islands. Fred would speak about defense, and Wally would speak about offense; sometimes, they would bring the wives along. We got to go to the small islands and the big islands. We would rent cars so that we could see some of the sites on all the islands.

One day, Wally and I went by ourselves in a rental car. He, being somewhat hardheaded, came to a DO NOT ENTER sign and ignored it. Soon, we were on a ledge on the face of the cliff which was approximately 15 feet wide! We were probably 100 feet above the ocean with no way to turn around. We just had to keep on going. It was a rough and rocky road. We probably traveled at least one half of a mile. I was petrified. Soon, we came to the end of it where we found ourselves in a native village. I will never forget the face of the lady who showed us how to get out of there. She had huge hands and high cheekbones. The Hawaiian people speak English with a different dialect. This lady was difficult to understand. She could understand us better than we could understand her.

Wally told her, "Thank you for helping us. Could you please point us in the direction of civilization?" She did, and we finally got home.

Downtown Honolulu is built between the ocean and the mountains. Many nice hotels and restaurants were built on level places carved out of rock. There are also many wonderful places to eat on wooden wharfs where you can eat out over the ocean.

There is also a wonderful Chinatown area in downtown Honolulu as well.

*****

The University of Hawaii plays footballs games in Aloha Stadium. We had been there before when we played in the Pro Bowl. Honolulu enjoys presenting the Pro Bowl. It brings a significant amount of business to that city. It also brings those very famous NFL pro football players, who bring their families along. Consequently, Honolulu attempts to make the visiting coaches and players very happy. They have festivities every night for the teams and coaches.

One of the evenings' entertainments took us to Don Ho's. You remember Don Ho? He was the guy that sang "Tiny Bubbles." Don Ho's is a really nice outdoor restaurant, and they have great food. Don Shula is a big soup lover. On the Dolphin training table in Miami, the Dolphins have soup offered every day. However, this was a new thing for Shula: I guess he rarely had the opportunity to eat vichyssoise, or cold potato soup. We were sitting near the Shulas, and I heard Shula call out, "Hey, waiter! My soup is cold!" Whereupon Bill Arnsparger and his wife, BJ, put their heads down and covered their mouths.

The waiter, being somewhat sophisticated, said, "Oh, I'm so sorry, Mr. Shula! We will heat that up for you right away!"

Now every time I see vichyssoise written on a menu, it prompts me to think of Don Shula and Don Ho's restaurant.

*****

Hawaii is different. The food is different, the culture is different, the scenery is different. You have the ocean and the mountains. There is wonderful fruit and delicious fresh seafood. There are different styles of cooking as well as different styles of serving. A luau is something special. The Hawaiian people enjoy socializing at luaus in their native dress.

Our son, Andrew, also enjoyed Hawaii. He attended St. Louis High School, which had won an unbelievable ten Hawaii State Championships in the prior eleven years. There are many Samoan young men who attended St. Louis High School. If you are not familiar with the Samoans, it is not unusual for one of their young men to grow to the size of 6'4" in height and over 300 pounds in weight. When Andrew was one of the quarterbacks, the St. Louis offensive line averaged 320 pounds per man.

The football season came, and Wally had a good experience with the offense coaching staff. Guy Benjamin (quarterback), Greg Olejack (offensive coordinator), Mike Green (wide receiver), and Don Dillon (running back) incorporated all the offensive ideas which had been so good to the teams where Wally had coached offenses before. The "check with me" system was as good for Tim Carey as it had been for all the quarterbacks who had preceded him in Wally's passing systems. The "check with me" system worked with Carey. Hawaii won six games and was within a point or two from winning three more. However, Wally wanted to coach Andrew.

Andrew's Football
Experience

Our fifth son, Andrew, probably has had the most unusual educational experience of all the sons. Wally wanted to coach him, so that led to Andrew enrolling at duPont Manual High School in Louisville, Kentucky, and starting his high school career with head coach Jerry Mays. Manual had been an outstanding high school football team in the 1930's – 60's and had won the National High School Football Championship six times. There were still some old-time Manual players around Louisville, such as Ray Bear, John Meihaus, and many others. Manual was also an outstanding baseball team. They had a great baseball diamond just behind the football stands. They seldom lost a baseball game.

Andrew got some experience as the junior varsity quarterback at Manual. Jerry Mays allowed Wally to put in the offense as well as coach Andrew. Manual High School had been a good starting place for Andrew. Andrew made great strides toward learning how to be a quarterback. Then in Texas at Wallis Orchard, he was the varsity quarterback. There was a good passing league in Texas. The Wallis Orchard team was not too good, but it was good quarterback experience.

When Fred von Appen hired Wally to be the offensive coordinator at the University of Hawaii, Andrew enrolled in St Louis High School, which was the old traditional high school in Honolulu. The sons of the old traditional Hawaiian families were allowed to attend the school tuition-free. There were only about ten Caucasian boys in St. Louis High School, and minorities were the white boys. They were looked down upon. In fact, the Hawaiian players would spit on the white boys as they walked to practice.

St. Louis had a really good Hawaiian coach named Cal Lee. Even though Andrew was a good developing quarterback, the two quarterbacks who were resident players at St. Louis were both major college prospects. They were ahead of him because they were familiar with the Cal Lee offense, so Andrew did the best he could and bided his time. Wally could see St. Louis was not the place for Andrew. Andrew needed to be the starter to get a college scholarship; after all, a college scholarship was worth $100,000. Wally started applying for high-school coaching jobs where he could coach Andrew.

CORNERSVILLE

We were finishing up at the University of Hawaii. We were looking for a place where Andrew could be the starting quarterback, so that he could get a scholarship. Wally really wanted a place where he could coach Andrew. He wrote letters to high schools who were looking for head coaches. He received a lot of replies, but it seemed there was always something that did not work for some reason. Finally, he received a favorable response for an athletic director in Tennessee at a place in Cornersville.

That athletic director said, "If you are in the Nashville area, our principal would like to visit with you about our football-coaching job."

So we went to Nashville, and Wally spoke to the lady principal and got the job.

We arrived in Cornersville, and Wally was introduced as the new coach at a pep rally in the auditorium. Cornersville had at one time had a strong high school athletic program but recently had fallen on hard times and replaced the coach who had preceded Wally. The community wanted a good program and was pleased to learn that Wally had a good coaching background. Practice started even before school officially opened. We rented a big house with a swimming pool. It had a large living room. Wally, in order to meet the parents and boosters, invited people to our house to view films of the game.

The parents and boosters liked Wally. However, Wally started an off-season conditioning and weight-lifting program, which Cornersville had never had. Then some of the baseball, track, and basketball players joined in the conditioning program, and their coaches went to the principal and board to complain.

Andrew was a senior and an all-state player. He was offered and accepted a scholarship to Marshall University in West Virginia, so our time at Cornersville, Tennessee, came to an end.

Part 2: Europe

Europe Preface

I would like to take you on our adventures in Europe: Italy, Germany, England, Spain, France, Serbia, and Hungary. John Grisham was right when he describes in *Playing for Pizza*, a book about playing American football in Europe, that that's the amount of salary you get: "enough to buy pizza."

When my husband coached for the Miami Dolphins, he met many European men interested in American football. The Dolphin training camp was a hub for visitors from around the world. When the Super Bowl was played in Miami, the Dolphins sponsored parties. One such party was on a boat with people from Europe who were interested in having teams over there. Wally met these men and kept their business cards; they always asked him if he would be interested in coaching in Europe. He always said yes.

In the '80s, American football was popping up in cities across Europe, mostly in Germany. There were American bases, and these men were wanting real football, not just soccer. TV brought an interest there also. Some of the soldiers played or coached the teams that started up.

Several years later, our phone rang. A voice, which I knew immediately was not speaking English, in broken words asked, "Isa da coach there-a?"

Wally started talking, and all I heard was, "Yes, yes, yes. Okay."

On the line was a man from Palermo, Sicily, wanting Wally to come and coach his team and teach them American football.

There was a great Italian restaurant nearby, and the owners were from Palermo. We visited them and called back to Sicily, and they interpreted for us. Thus began our trek to Europe.

Erice and Palermo, Sicily: 1989

Our first stop in Europe was Palermo, Sicily. I have always been interested in history, and while traveling in Europe, we were surrounded by it. Wally and Dan flew ahead to get ready for our first game, against Trapani. Tommy and Andrew, two of our sons, were to follow with me in a few weeks. When we landed in Rome to change planes to Sicily, there were armed guards in the airport with M1 rifles. We certainly did not see this in America. This was 1989, and the boys were all hyped up about the guns and the soldiers. We were very quiet as we made our way to Alitalia, the Italian airline. As we boarded the plane, we noticed people carrying babies, very large bundles, bread and wine, and I believe a few chickens. No one spoke English, and we were the country bumpkins in our nice, bright American clothes. The Italians all wore black. The people could not have been nicer. We were able to communicate because they wanted to share their food with us. Wally had called and told us the football field in Palermo was just dirt and rocks, and it was surrounded by bombed-out buildings from World War II. What we learned along the way was, you never knew how good the facilities were going to be. In America, we always had good facilities and places to play, but in Europe, you did the best you could with what you were given.

When we first arrived in Italy, we were picked up at the airport by players of the Palermo Cardinals, who stuffed our bags into their cars and whisked us away to practice. We started putting in the offense as the first matter of business. Our son, Dan, was there and knew the offensive terminology, so he could call the plays in the huddle. The days went by, and soon it was time for the first game. It was on the road. The team traveled by bus. It took approximately one hour to get to Trapani. There was a nice soccer stadium there. The visitor dressing room was up a long flight of stairs. There was a caretaker in the dressing room. He told us that this place, called Erice, had been the headquarters for Benito Mussolini during the war. He was called "il Duce," or "the leader."

Erice was a small, walled town with a long history. In Roman days, it had been a fertility castle for Potnia, a fertility goddess. A nobleman named Erix was buried there after losing a boxing match to Hercules and died, so Erice was a famous place.

Wally and Dan came down to the playing field. Some American soldiers were the officials for the game. After the first quarter, the score was 28–0 in favor of Palermo.

The officials called Wally over and said, "Please, Coach, tell me this is not going to be a 100–0 game."

At the half, it was 48–0. Wally told Dan to run basic plays; however, the Cardinals scored thirty points on defense, so the end score was 88–0. After the game, Wally and Dan went into a restaurant to get some dinner. They ordered and got the bill, which was eighty-eight euros. Another group from Palermo had basically the same meal, and their invoice was nineteen euros. Later, Wally and Dan found out the restaurant owner was also a Trapani coach, so their eighty-eight euros bill was probably due to the eighty-eight points they scored in the football game.

Our apartment overlooked the Mediterranean from the balcony, but it was not the villa I had expected. Most people would say "Wonderful! This is an adventure!" We had two dorm-sized rooms that consisted of bunk beds for the boys in one room and a pull-out couch for Wally and me in the other room. We had a connecting door, a very small icebox, a stove, a sink, and a small shower room. There was only enough food for one day in the icebox, so we walked to the village each day to shop. We got to know all the shop people in the seaside village of Mondello. I kept telling myself that some people save all their lives to come to this beautiful place. I later found out there were beautiful villas and larger apartments that we could've had, but Wally felt that this was the safest place. It was the only place that was totally enclosed by a wall, and the only way in was through a guarded gate. At that time in Palermo, the Mafia and the court judges were at war. Several judges had convicted Mafia people and put them in jail. In our quiet seaside town lived several judges. The first morning we were there, we walked to town. I noticed the tanks in the street in front of the judges' homes along with armed guards. This is how I found out why we lived where we lived. You had to jog around the tanks to get to the next street to shop. At first, the soldiers would say "Alt [Stop]!" until we became a common everyday occurrence to them as we traveled to the grocery or for our morning coffee and delicious cornettoes, which is a pastry filled with cream and chocolate.

Not having any idea what things cost and no knowledge of lira—Italy's currency at the time—we were on a very tight budget. Our airfare had been paid for, and our apartment was paid for, but our salary was very meager for five people to live on. We had to pay for our own food, so we did most of our dinners by cooking in the apartment. Living in the next apartment was a lovely Italian lady named Tammy who took a liking to us. Tammy would climb over her balcony onto ours several mornings a week just to see what Wally was cooking. She would go to the mari—the ocean—daily, and she would bring us fresh fish. Tammy then would tell Wally how to cook it, or she would come into our kitchen to see what we were cooking and tell Wally what he was doing wrong. We were always cooking and eating on the balcony or hanging our clothes out to dry. She was a funny and delightful neighbor.

The boys were the hit of the complex. They had brought their Nintendo, so all the little Italian boys would come to our apartment to play. It was amazing how these boys communicated. They really had a lot of fun playing the game, The Legend of Zelda. My boys made a deck of cards from cardboard and worked on a monopoly set, but we found the dice too expensive.

We went to the beach every day. Picture a half circle of mountains surrounding the beautiful blue Mediterranean. The Italians had little sheds that they rented by the month. They could change their clothes and keep their food in these sheds. They never went anywhere without food. The beach was lined with these little houses. We didn't have to rent one because we lived right off the sea.

I called my mom and dad every Sunday. After our first phone conversation, Dad got the message that money was tight, so he sent me a check for five hundred dollars. When I went to the bank to exchange it, I walked into a room where I was searched with an electronic device, and then I was allowed into the bank. It took several days to get the money, but when I did, I felt rich. I think I got two million liras, a vast amount for my American dollars.

We had a rickety, old car, which we often had to push to get started. A new car in Italy would have been ruined in no time. Drivers did not heed any signs, and there were no stoplights. It took courage to drive in Mondello. Going to practice was like riding on a roller coaster: you held on for dear life! Practice was three times a week, and then we played the game on Saturday or Sunday. The team would all go out for pizza after the games. This was a treat for us because the team paid for the pizza.

We had a good team. Wally was coaching, and Danny was quarterback. American football became the rage in Palermo. We won every game. Our total score for the ten games was 620 to the opponents' 52. Danny passed at least fifty times a game. When he passed the ball, the crowd hollered, "Dannie, Dannieeee, Dannieee." They loved the pass. The other teams in Italy did not do much passing; they were just developing the running game. At one such win, the president of the Calgary Italian Sportsmen's Dinner Association, Domenic Venturo—also owner of team—asked to speak to the team. Wally, of course, agreed. He could not understand what Mr. Venturo was saying, so he asked a team member who spoke English to translate.

The player said, "Quiet, he is speaking."

After the talk, the player said, "Mr. Venturo said that we are all brothers. We are all Italians, and we are all Catholic. We are all friends. It will not be necessary to beat this team 100–0. 60 to nothing will be okay." Wally choked on his salami sandwich.

The Italian teams were just starting to play American football, so Wally's experience as a professional coach with ten years in the NFL and eight Division 1 Colleges were a huge advantage to the Italian football program. In addition to his coaching experience, he had been personally involved with designing some of the best offensive football schemes to be used by teams in America.

Our second road game that year took us by bus to Catania, which was about three hours from Palermo. Wally asked Mr. Venturo if we could stop along the way for our pregame meal. I had noticed many cars following us. Since this was my first away game, I was not sure if people would come or not. About halfway to the game, the bus pulled over to a roadside park. All the cars did the same. Within minutes, the mothers had a lavish picnic setup with wine. We ate pasta, which we didn't realize in Italy is considered the first course.

Wally, thinking that the meal was over, got up and proceeded to give his pep talk and shouted, "Let's go!"

...to which we heard an arousing cry, "No! No! More food!" from the mothers.

We finished the meal, wine and all, in about two hours. Wally was about to have a heart attack. We were an hour late for the game. He figured the team would be so full they would not be able to play without cramps. We won the game 72–6. Wally never complained again about the food. It seemed to be an Italian kind of thing, and we adjusted to it.

While we lived in Sicily, we had a water shortage. We could only use the water for twenty minutes in the morning and twenty minutes in the evening. We washed our clothes in a bucket and the dishes in the sink in the morning. The boys, Wally, and I were each allowed three minutes for a shower at night.

One of the players mentioned a spa near his seaside home in Mondello. I could not wait: a real bath! I was very excited. We drove to his home on a Sunday for a typical Italian meal. The first course was pasta with whole baby squid and black ink for topping. I kindly asked for the red sauce. The second course was leg-of-lamb, vegetable salad, and hot, fresh bread. Finally, we had dessert, which was fresh fruit, cream caramel, pastries, and coffee. (I gained twenty pounds while we were there. I love Italy.) After the meal, all the players said, "Let's go up to the spa." I could not wait.

We drove up the mountain about five miles. The cars in front of us pulled over. All the players and my sons piled out and ran down a dirt path covered with a canopy of trees and flowers. My thoughts at this moment were that this must be a really special spa as I walked the path. It had to be something special way up here. When I turned the last curve of the path, I saw two large water holes, more like two ponds, only filled with muddy water. There was a spurt of water shooting up about one foot above the water holes. It streamed down a slippery path into the ponds. My boys were up there getting ready to slide down what I called a mountain. I took the plunge. The water was hot, and if you rubbed the mud on your skin, it was very soothing. Afterward, my skin felt like silk. I overheard some of the players telling Danny this was a great place to bring a girl.

Because of the football schedule, we played a game each weekend. The island of Sicily is approximately five hundred kilometers around. Traveling was the best part of the job. We drove to every corner of this interesting island. Sicily has been occupied by 32 different countries. It seemed there are more Greek ruins in Sicily than in Greece, many as spectacular as the Parthenon. In Palermo, there was evidence of the Norman invasion: a magnificent castle. There were Gothic churches and medieval churches. Their architecture abounds in the city. Arabic mosaics; Roman walls. The walking tour took us all over downtown and old town. These places were still lived in.

After one game, we traveled to Selinunte. It had been a fort city, as it was on the southern Mediterranean coast facing Africa, an excellent vantage point overlooking the sea. The ruins that were left in the city were minimal: mostly stones, a few granite bathtubs, walls, and chairs. To me, the most exciting thing about this city was that Hannibal was there riding on his elephants when he fought in Sicily. There were no gates; you could just walk around and see the remains. I take a small rock from every place we have visited. I suppose some of these rocks were parts of old buildings, possibly a thousand years old. I have quite a collection.

Each weekend after a team win, Mr. Venturo always took us to a special restaurant. After one game, we went to a restaurant that served homemade pasta; this pasta had lobster tails with lobster sauce.

The following week, we went to Agrigento, a small, picturesque town in the mountains called the "Valley of the Temples." Can you imagine how much all this traveling would have cost the five of us? Even though the pay was minimal, the travel was top notch. After winning this game only 56–7 (the defense let us down), we toured the city. That trip was fantastic. It was so beautiful; it would be one that would be seen on a picture postcard. The perfect old city had narrow streets weaving their way through, cobblestone steps, and buildings put together with mud and sticks still standing. Most of the stadiums in these cities were fairly new, as American football was just coming into being. These were soccer stadiums originally; now many of the larger cities in Italy have their own football stadiums.

We were fortunate to spend the weekend in Agrigento. It was Easter weekend. Easter Sunday is one of the biggest days in Italy. We were able to see a parade where many football players were involved. They carried a statue of Madonna carrying a crucifix. The whole town participated. Small girls wore white dresses. It reminded me of a scene from the movie *The Godfather*. Profuse flowers: the perfume from the flowers permeated the city. There was joyful singing and bright clothes; normally people wore black, but not on this day. The best was yet to come: the food. The team, the president, and our family were treated royally.

The next week, we drove west to a game in Syracuse. We drove through wheat fields as far as the eye could see. Olive trees were planted right up the side of the mountains so high, I wondered how they ever got up there to plant them, cultivate them, and pick them. This area was the center of Sicily and was called the Breadbasket of Rome. At the time of the Roman Empire, they supplied all of Rome with wheat wine and lemons as big as apples. Large ships would carry all these staples up the Mediterranean to the mouth of the Tiber River, where they were put on small ships that took them up to Rome, about fifteen miles. An archaeologist told me that some of the ships that sank had been found with large jars of wine and olive oil that were still intact.

The owner of the team, Mr. Venturo, invited our family to see all these places. Through football, I got an education, learning how the Sicilians lived. We became part of a family. The three months we were there was the trip of a lifetime. We could never have afforded such a trip. The team learned American football. We won all the games, which my husband would tell you was the most important thing; I might have to disagree. Because of the winning season, we were offered three coaching jobs for the next year: Rome, Parma, and Bolzano. We visited Bolzano and Rome. The interview in Rome included housing and food, a tour of the Vatican, and all.

Birmingham, England

After having coached the Palermo Cardinals to the national championship, and after being noticed as someone who could bring another team to a championship, Wally was contacted by Birmingham in England, who had an owner and general manager who wanted to be one of the best teams in Europe. David Webb was the police chief in Birmingham, England, and was interested in American football. Mr. Webb was interested in sports of all kinds. He had been to Louisville to admire Muhammad Ali up close as the heavyweight boxing champion of the world. Wally had met David informally at a boxing ceremony in Louisville. I had a function for Muhammad and his wife, Lonnie, at a Derby party. David invited Wally to come and coach with the Birmingham Bulls in Birmingham, England.

Wally was really surprised by the quality of players Birmingham had. Mr. Webb really wanted to win and had made arrangements to bring players from London to Birmingham to practice and play. NFL Europe (originally World League of American Football) had just disbanded, so many of their players were available. David had gotten them committed to play for the Birmingham Bulls. I put together a lot of NFL T-shirts and some

NFL jewelry to sell at the Bulls games. We made good profits, as I recall.

Wally had talked our son, Jon, into being the quarterback for the Bulls. Jon and Wally went to England first. The owner of the team gave us a nice flat and a nice 4-door Ford sedan to use. The Bulls had some good players; however, so did the London Monarchs team. Both teams played through an undefeated season and were 12–0. Coming into the final game, Jon, our son, had been one of the outstanding players in the league, as had the Bulls' running back. They both had contract offers from the Oakland Raiders and the New York Jets. London also had good players, mostly on defense. The game day came, and the game was in progress. At the half, London was ahead 14–12, but Birmingham came back and won 19–14. Jon, after throwing two touchdown passes, was voted the outstanding player in the game. After the game, Wally, Andrew, and I returned to Louisville. We were quiet for a short time, until someone else from Europe called, and once again we were off.

England was so good because everyone spoke English. I remember Andrew saying as we got off the boat from France, "I'm so glad we are here [in England]. I could not understand those people over there."

Driving on the left side of the road was very difficult. I did not drive because of driving on the left side. Jon and Wally drove us everywhere. Andrew and I could walk most places, so while Wally and Jon worked on football, Andrew and I played.

Also, names of things there are different. The best grocery was Sainsbury's. It was just like our groceries, only, if I asked for cookies, they were called biscuits, and if I asked for beer, it was called a pint. They would laugh at me in the grocery store. They thought I talked funny because of my southern accent and because of the funny things I asked for. In the heart of Birmingham, England, was what they called the Bull Ring; at one time, that is what it was. Now it is a huge shopping center: we could buy anything. The prices were reasonable, only we paid with the pound. One dollar would be worth about £0.75. Trying to figure it out took some getting used to.

Andrew and I got to fly from Birmingham to Paris, France. Every Monday on TV in England, they would advertise round trips for $89—this included airfare, hotel for five days, and a bus ticket to travel around Paris. One of the players did this and told us about it, so off Andrew and I went to Paris! All because of traveling with the coach: not many people get to fly to Paris for $89.

We loved England.

Deggendorf, Germany

Our son, Tom, was the quarterback for the Deggendorf team. Andrew also went with us. We won all the games and were able to travel all over southern Germany. We saw the Eagle's Nest, or Hitler's hideout, in Berchtesgaden. We were able to go to a spa in the Black Forest, in Baden-Baden. In the spa, the thing that struck me as funny was the Muslim men walked around with just a little jock strap, but the women were covered from head to toe.

Munich, Germany

We were in Munich for one season for the Munich Cowboys. We had a very nice apartment in a hotel. We could get on the streetcar and travel all over the city with one ticket. We could get off and on as many times as we wanted. We had free food at a wonderful German restaurant right by our apartment. We always got breakfast at the hotel where we lived. The team always had beer and sausage after practice.

We had a great car and drove all over Germany. We went to Berlin and saw the Berlin Wall and Checkpoint Charlie, the crossing point between East and West Germany. We drove into Poland and saw concentration camps. From the top of Germany, from Hamburg, we took a ferry over to Denmark. We drove to Sweden then back to the ferry and back to Munich. All this because of football and traveling with the coach.

Amiens, France

Amiens, France, was a nice, quiet little town near the border of Belgium. Many First World War battles were fought near Amiens by American, French, Australian, and Canadian soldiers versus the Germans. Amiens was important as a Second World War battle site, and many sites were considered historical landmarks. Some of the surrounding towns had hosted the biggest battles of World War I and World War II: Dunkirk, Calais, and Cherbourg were only a short drive from Amiens.

We traveled all over France. We could drive anywhere. I can remember one Sunday after an Amiens game, we had driven to Bruges, Belgium, to recruit a player. On our return to Amiens, it was obvious how much preparation the Germans had done for war. As we returned to Amiens along the English Channel, there were stone walls where there had been large cannons and anti-aircraft guns. It might not have been smart, but we stopped and got out of our car and went inside some of the German bunkers. They were serious about repelling any aggression from England just across the channel, a straight shot over the white cliffs of Dover. The Germans had gun emplacements all along the Belgian/French side of the English Channel. However, these many years after the war, life was going on as if nothing happened.

We were ninety kilometers from Paris. We drove all over France from top to bottom: Champagne country to the French

Riviera. Boulogne and Abbeville were vibrant little seaside towns with brightly clad citizens hustling around looking for a place to eat. I can still recall their bright clothing. The Amiens stores were greatly influenced by Paris because Paris was so close. Beauvais, Compiègne, and Reims were also nearby. Back in Amiens, there are good restaurants on the Somme River, which divides the city. We saw the Jules Vern house on 2 Rue Charles Dubois in Amiens.

We had an apartment over a sports school and a culinary school. The players could all go to sports school. We had three meals a day at the culinary school, wine with every meal, and wonderful food. My blood was made thin by too much wine and fresh tomatoes. We found a small French restaurant we loved to eat at on our outings; because we were Americans, they were exceptionally nice. They would take Wally to the kitchen and show him all kinds of French food. We could walk all over Amiens, but at night, we noticed everything shut down at dark.

France won the national championship. The team won and danced in a line saying, "No bullshit!" This is what Wally told them every day at practice: "No bullshit."

Rome, Italy

Wally coached the Rome team. We lived in a nice apartment with a large living room, bath, and bedroom. We were given money for food, so we did very little cooking. We had a great car and could drive into the city, about ten kilometers from our house. We ate our way through Rome. Fettucine in Italy is a lot better than in America.

We went to Mass at St. Peter's Basilica. We drove the Appian Way to a spa that was built by Emperor Hadrian for his generals, the Hadrianic Baths. The architecture and the arches were amazing and still intact. We went to the oldest city where the Tiber River started. This river goes directly to the city of Rome. Ships would come up the Mediterranean from Sicily, unload at the Tiber, and then barges shipped the goods up to the city.

All the ruins of their city were well intact. We went to the Colosseum; we drove to Florence; we drove to Naples. We saw the ruins of the city of Pompeii, which was destroyed by a volcano. What an education, all for free, because of traveling with the coach.

We lived near a beautiful park, which we walked through each day to have breakfast. People recognized Wally and would always try to talk to him about the football team. One of the owners of the team was a pilot for Alitalia Airline. He flew us to Dubai for a weekend (free, of course).

We practiced three times a week and played our games on Sunday. I got to shop with some of the owners' wives while the team practiced. Not a day went by that we did not travel to one amazing ruin after another.

When someone invited us to dinner at their house, I knew I was in for a treat. The first course was always pasta, then meat and vegetables, then salad, and at last, fruit and cake. I gained twenty pounds.

We won all our games. The team gave Wally a beautiful watch.

Barcelona, Spain

While we coached in Rome, we played a team from Barcelona, Spain. After the season in Rome, the team from Spain called and asked Wally to coach their team the next year. Again, we were given plane tickets, food allowance, and a small salary and great car.

We traveled from the top of Spain to the bottom. Once while driving in the Pyrenees Mountains near Lourdes, France, I asked Wally if we could drive to Fátima, Portugal, to a Catholic shrine that I thought was only about another hundred miles across Spain. (It's over 670 miles.) We arrived at night. It was beautiful: the people were having a candlelight procession to the church, and all were singing. I did not know I could take Holy Water if I wanted to, so I did not have a container to put some water in. Wally went into the men's restroom and paid the janitor for one of his bottles. We filled it with the Holy Water, and I brought it back to America. I give some to anyone who is ill.

We won all our games. We ate many different foods and saw it all.

Belgrade, Serbia: 2008

Serbia was definitely a third-world country. When I arrived from London, I was met by armed men as we exited be plane. Many different languages were spoken, none familiar to me. As we drove from the airport, I knew it was definitely not like Italy, England, Spain, or Germany. Much graffiti on the walls of buildings, poor street signs, and the Audubon was nonexistent. That Wally would not drive here, you must know it was bad, as he had driven all over Europe.

We lived in an apartment that had bullet holes in the walls. The Americans had bombed this area; the football players said they could sit on their roofs and watch the smart bombs dive into exact targets. We would walk to lunch each day from our apartment. May 1, May Day, they had a big holiday, and lots of people were picnicking. As we walked, we saw a man with a large side of lamb on a spit. As we walked by, we said hello and asked about the lamb. The man had a large knife; we were not sure as he approached us if he was friend or foe. They were not happy with America. The man came over and grabbed Wally's arm and said, "Have some of the lamb." He could not have been nicer.

The people were excellent. Young people were joyous and happy. Old people seemed grim in their dark clothes. Our apartment was fine, in a nice area, but if we were living in the US, you would think we were living in the ghetto.

After being here a few days, I marveled at people's tenacity. Despite all of the wars, they had hope, and I saw progress. I did not realize it had been part of the Ottoman Empire for five hundred years, until 1886. From then, they were wrecked with war by Germany, Russia, the United States, Great Britain, and others, yet they survived with a great attitude. A man named Bora, our driver, was very intelligent, very knowledgeable of history, and was up to date on this country.

This was nothing like the rest of Europe; someone must have drawn a line between Italy, Germany, Austria, and some of the other countries' thriving, progressive metropolises. Overall, it was a great experience.

MARCH 2008

The more I learned about this country, the more I liked it. It's a small country, about 500 miles long and 300 miles wide. They stood alone against the Ottoman Empire. They have been through many cruel occupations worse than the German people. The Serbians love food, like the Italians do, and are very family-oriented, always gathering together for an occasion with lots of food. There was not much to see in this country: no ruins left over from the Ottoman Empire. There were a lot of new buildings going up everywhere. They had five or six large shopping centers. This seemed to be a simple country. The people lived in poverty but drove cars.

APRIL 2008

It was a very nice spring. Everything was blossoming out. When we sat in the dining room at the Trim restaurant, we could be sitting in our own dining room looking out at the view. We went downtown, where I shopped at an open-air market with wonderful vegetables and fruits. They had some clothes, reasonably priced. Wally paid three euros for a clock battery at a jewelry store, but we probably could have gotten it at the open-air market for one euro.

People there were a lot like our son, Jon: nice and kind to people, never meeting a stranger, just a new friend.

Downtown had beautiful wide streets, good but expensive shops, and walking zones. There were many bombed-out buildings in the middle of town. One home on a hill away from town was not bombed; I do not know why.

We had our first game. The field was too short, so they put the 40-yard markers five yards from the 50-yard marker. The grass was high. It was a good game. In the last few minutes, the other team led 32–28, but we led the whole way until then. These kids were pretty good. Some had never played football before. Wally had done a good job teaching them. He worked very hard.

There were lots of young families out everywhere with lots of children. Serbians were under communist rule until 1992, and there were still many signs of it. The cleaning lady made the same money as the boss, but she could not tell anyone what to do. Pretty soon, people said, "I am working so hard when someone who is not working as hard gets the same pay," so people just stopped working. I was told a lot of people here did not work. I don't know where their money came from because everywhere you looked, people were shopping, eating, or out to sporting events, spending money. At an excellent grocery, it was packed. An equivalent to Walmart was packed at 3:00 in the afternoon, and people were in all the downtown restaurants and stores.

We went to a Serbian restaurant and had beer in mugs like in Hanover, Germany. It was a beautiful little restaurant named The Bears; they wore the costume of the country. They had live Fanta chickens running around on the floor. The decor was vintage. With Serbia being established in the fifteenth to sixteenth century, one part of the restaurant was very old with wooden walls. They had added a new section. Old things hung on the walls: spoons, pots, etc. It really was a very good place, just funny with all the chickens. It was five-star, very elegant. A band serenaded us, and people sat around and sang. The street was cobblestone: only walking, no car traffic. This was a very old part of Belgrade, probably the oldest part. We always walked to lunch and dinner. There was a beautiful park that we walked through: in the middle of it, we couldn't see anything else except forest. The forest was so thick, like in Deggendorf.

We went to a scrimmage a hundred miles away; there was nothing between Belgrade and that city. No ruins. Members of the team remembered watching the smart bombs being hurled into the city. They told us how they went up to the top of their building and watched the war.

There was a Roman fort on the hill, it overlooked where the Danube went. Belgrade is a beautiful city downtown with wide streets, old buildings, with original brick streets, wonderful restaurants, singing groups, and excellent food. But there were still signs of the war, even in our apartment building.

Back to England, then Italy

The bombs were falling on the American Embassy in Belgrade, or at least I thought they were. It turned out they set the embassy on fire. I believed it was time to leave.

Wally got online and made a few calls. Wally called Sicily to see if they still needed a coach. They said, "Don't go home. Come here."

Another team in Birmingham, England, wanted Wally to come for a visit. We went to England, landed, and got the bus to Birmingham at the Airport. We made a call to our connection, Andy, who had suggested we call him at home, where we would be staying. He met us; he was a very large man, and he said that he helped the team. We would be staying there for three days. It appeared to be a poor neighborhood, but what could we do?

At three in the morning, we went and took three flights of stairs to a clean bathroom down the hall. We had four bags, which we left on the first floor, hoping to see them in the morning. No soap there, but at least there was hot water.

When we got up in the morning, we spent the day downtown. We called our friend, David Web; he's a lifesaver. That night, Wally went to meet the team management. They were a no-show, but someone came and took us out for pizza. Web, former owner of the Bulls, where Wally had coached previously, took us to lunch the next day and dinner at a soccer club. We met with his rotary club; it was very nice. Wally went to meet with the team management who were again no-shows.

Wally never did meet with them and never got money for the trip as promised, so we decided to head back to Italy thanks to David. David Web was a true gentleman; we were fortunate that we knew him. He got us tickets out of Heathrow, where we found we had too many suitcases for the trip out. We had to sit on the floor in the middle of the airport and dump out clothes to take to Italy. We were only allowed one bag, 25 kg. Again, thanks to David, we shipped the other two bags back to Birmingham, England, where they still were three years later. If we had taken the bags to Italy, it would have cost nine hundred euros.

Palermo, Sicily: 2008

I was afraid when we pulled up in front of the apartment that Wally would have a fit; it sounded like we had a third-floor apartment, and the neighborhood didn't look too good. Wally made a few noises as we went inside. It was a very nice first floor living room, office, and small kitchen. There was a spiral stair-case to the second floor, with a large bedroom and bath, and a third floor eating area, toilet, washer, and a wonderful deck over-looking the mountains and ocean. Back in May of 1989, the first time we went to Palermo, we had dorm-sized rooms: one for Wally and me, and one for Dan, Tom, and Andrew, with smaller showers. We had water ten minutes a day because of the water shortage. We overlooked the Mediterranean, but that was an-other story.

In 2008, this was fun. We lived half a block off the main street of the little town, half a mile from the ocean. In Mandela, a Rome commune, all knew Wally was the coach, so everyone spoke to him and made signals to him. The old Italian men stood around and talked with sign language. We bought a book to un-derstand these signs.

We could walk everywhere. There was a great pizza place that the American football player Vinny Testaverde's family supposedly owned. We got to know a lot of people on the small street, so we felt like a part of the place. We could get everything from bathing suits, sunglasses, and ice cream to fresh fruits and vegetables, meat, and coffee. There were small shops for six blocks. We also had vendors coming around every day yelling to buy their vegetables, fruit, and fish. We bought a large frying pan in the street. We walked every day to shop and buy groceries. A shop van pulled up outside of our home and slid open its side, revealing a meat and cheese store. Little kids rode around on what we used to call an ice cream bicycle to sell espressos.

We ate at a fabulous Mexican restaurant, not like we have in the U.S. The lamb chops were the best that I had ever eaten.

The first time I ever called Wally at the football field was when I broke my wrist in Italy. I stayed overnight at the Italian hospital. There were no rolls of toilet paper, washcloths, or towels there; you had to ask for them. I was in a ward full of old Italian women who spoke no English. They cried all night and talked.

I called my son, "Dr. Steve," and told him.

He said, "Come home; don't let them do anything."

I told Wally to get me out of there. When I got back to the U.S., I told everyone I fell while dancing in a fountain, which sounded a lot better than falling off a chair in the computer store.

A TRIP TO FRANCE

We got a car in France. We traveled all over, places out of the way, like medieval cities. A chef served wonderful food twice every day. A friend took us to Amiens, and we got to know the avenues. There was an open-air market.

We saw wonderful old chateaus, explored the countryside, and went through all the wine country. We ate at many pubs, always downstairs, underground. People had shops and restaurants with apartments on the floors above. In the spring, people start to have outside seating. It was very nice.

Bolzano, Italy: 2010

In the Bolzano-Italian Alps, we had a very small apartment, like a hotel room. There was a great restaurant where we ate each day. It was breathtaking scenery with snowcapped mountains. There were fruit trees everywhere. On the side of the mountains, grapes. A picture everywhere you look. Every sign was written in both Italian and English.

There's much Austrian influence in Northern Italy. Just below Austria, it has totally different architecture than Southern Italy. It all looked like a postcard out our window, the most beautiful place we have lived. We could see valleys, green trees, flowers, plants, everything in bloom, guarded by towering mountains. Forst Beer brewery is there in the mountains; they use mountain water. There were houses on a mountain switchback—we couldn't look down. Finally, we got over the Alps. We spent a day sightseeing in the Alps.

April 25 is a holiday there, Liberation Day, the unification of the two sides of Italy. On this day, they overcame Nazi Germany and the Italian Social Republic. They hold many parties and a parade. We were invited to everything, and there was lots of food, dancing, and singing.

Budapest, Hungary

There we were in Budapest, Hungary. What in the world were we doing there? We asked ourselves that question every time we moved someplace. Our experience here in Hungary was great, next to Italy.

I loved it there. There was so much to do. It was very inexpensive: you could get a massage for 3,000 Ft, or forints, Hungarian money that was equal to ten euros or about U.S. $12.00. I could fix my hair for about 2,000 Ft / seven Euros / $8.00. The old buildings there were magnificent. Budapest at one time was a wealthy city. Previously separate were Buda on the hill on one side of the Danube River and Pest on the flat side of the Danube.

We had a nice apartment, two bedrooms and two baths. We were given a place to eat dinner at night and money for food for lunch and breakfast. The food was great: chicken paprikash, Hungarian stew, all you could eat. We had a kitchen with everything, even a washer-dryer combination. There were Saturday games, and we would practice three times a week. We were one stop away from the trolleybus line. On Sundays, there were no games; we could get on the trolleybus and go around the whole city on Sundays. The Hungarians were big on festivals on Sundays: lots of wine tasting and food tasting on the street, so we would go from festival to festival and eat and drink free. They had a magnificent opera house. Wally and I were given free tickets to attend.

At the end of our boulevard was a five-star hotel and restaurant. They had hot thermal baths that anyone could pay to go in, so while Wally was at practice, I would go to the baths. These were nude baths, but women were on one side and then the men had their place. I never saw so many out-of-shape women in the nude in all my life. The baths were wonderful. They had one that was very hot and one that was okay. I had no aches or pains while in Hungary.

We did not get paid much money in Europe, but we got our plane fare, food, apartment, and a little salary, enough to enjoy the sights. You could get on a small boat and cruise on the Danube; we were able to see all of Europe from the top of Germany to the bottom of Spain: Portugal, France, Italy, Serbia, Hungary, and Yugoslavia. We saw it all.

May 1st is Labor Day, a holiday in Europe, a great day. Thousands were in the park where we walked each day to get our meal at The Spot. People were cooking a whole lamb, and it was homemade with a big stick from mouth to rear of lamb. We stopped to talk; some spoke English, and they gave us some lamb. It was delicious. One man was at each end of it, turning it over a fire. Another group was toasting drinks and eating pickled colored eggs. They gave us a drink to toast and eggs to eat. They took Wally's arms in theirs and gave a toast to America, then downed the hot plum drink.

Conclusion

We would normally go to Europe in February or March. The football season started at the end of March and finished at the end of June, so we were always home by the Fourth of July.

After fifty years of coaching, my husband retired. He did clinics for several years after he retired; people still called him coach.

We were married for sixty-five years. I traveled with the coach all those years.

Perks: Coaches get a lot of perks, so the wives get to enjoy them also. We always got a new car to drive. Wally had a TV show and a radio show as a coach. He chose to take trade outs instead of money, which meant we could go to restaurants that were his sponsors' and eat free.

He had a florist for a sponsor, so I always had fresh flowers in the house. At Christmastime, I got a beautiful Christmas tree, and the florist decorated it. Two of his sponsors were Eastern Airlines and Marriott Hotels. We took the whole family to Europe, flew free, and stayed at hotels free. There was also a men's clothing store; Wally got free clothes. Another was a jewelry store; I got a beautiful diamond bracelet.

The downside: Coaches work fourteen hours a day and sometimes more, seven days a week. There were times when Wally would not see the boys for two weeks because he would leave before they got up and not get home till after they were asleep. Or he was on the road recruiting football players.

Coaches' wives are a special breed; I would not trade our lives for anything. I have gotten to do more things that most people could never do because of traveling with the coach.

About the Author

Peggy English is a mother of five sons and a wife of sixty-five years. She traveled around the world with her husband, Wally, and she would not trade their life together for anything. She has been very blessed.